# SILENCE IN HEAVEN

## A SURVEY OF THE BOOK OF REVELATION

D1795513

I would like to dedicate this work to Gillian, friend of Hobbits, who met me as a student atheist and reintroduced me to the Christian faith.

# SILENCE IN HEAVEN

## A SURVEY OF THE BOOK OF REVELATION

# STEPHEN DISRAELI

**Library of Congress Catalog Number: 2021951902**
Disraeli, Stephen, Author
*Silence in Heaven*, by Stephen Disraeli
Advantage Books, Longwood, FL, 2022
ISBN (print): 9781597556736
(ePub):9781597556811


First Printing: February 2022
21 22 23 24 25 26 27 10 9 8 7 6 5 4 3 2 1

# Table of Contents

*Stephen Disraeli*

# FOREWORD

The Book of Revelation is "a call for the endurance and faith of the saints".

That is, the book is addressing the fears of a church experiencing intense persecution. That church needs to stay focused on its trust in God, resisting the temptation to despair. The purpose of Revelation is to encourage them and motivate them to remain faithful.

But which church? On the one hand, the immediate answer would have to be "the church of the Roman empire". Like every other prophet in the Bible, John is addressing the people of his own time, in the first instance. When he speaks to them in the first chapter, he says "I share with you the tribulation and the patient endurance." Their bad experience began with Nero's vindictive treatment of the Christians in Rome (A.D.64) and came to a climax in the grand campaign (A.D. 302-311) set in motion by Diocletian. John will be referring to Nero's persecution, or to something a little later like the troubles of Domitian's reign.

On the other hand, the vision itself is describing God's reaction to the persecution. In other words, looking into John's future. Clearly the bulk of what the vision foresees has not been fulfilled, even in metaphor. In particular, nobody can claim that we are living in the "new Jerusalem" of the last two chapters. So it is reasonable to suppose, as many people do suppose, that John is addressing a crisis-troubled church of the future.

I believe the answer to the conundrum is that John is addressing both churches at the same time. There are two troubled Christian communities, two oppressive regimes, two periods of tribulation, and two triumphant victories of God over a persecuting world. One set for the church of the Roman empire, and the other set for the future church.

That answer is also the key to understanding what the book of Revelation says. The God of the Bible is a communicating God. He wants people to understand him. If this book was given as a message for the church of John's time, then it should have been possible, in principle, for the church of John's time to grasp its basic meaning. Otherwise, they would get no benefit. So what makes it difficult for modern readers to grasp that basic message? What's missing, in our case?

One factor is the difference in situation. Let me offer an analogy. In the days when I was commuting into London, I frequently found myself standing near a notice which began with the unsettling words "It is usually safer to remain on the train." If I had taken that warning literally, keeping still and waiting for further advice from railway staff, I would never have reached my destination. Reading between the lines, though (and remembering other notices on other trains), I could recognize the suppressed opening clause; "In the event of an accident or other emergency…" In other words, the message was not really meant for me. It was meant for future passengers in different circumstances.

At the time of writing, we in the modern church are living in the comparatively peaceful interval between the tribulation imposed by the Roman empire and the tribulation imposed by the Beast. So the message of Revelation, addressed to a church in tribulation, cannot be understood by us without an effort of the imagination. We must put ourselves in their place in order to perceive the central theme of Revelation, namely God's faithful response to the world's oppression of the church.

Another factor is that the church of John's time were probably more at home in the Old Testament scriptures than the average modern Christian. That was a vital advantage, because the message of Revelation is carried by the overtones of its imagery, an imagery borrowed extensively from the Old Testament. This turns the Old Testament into a kind of code-book for Revelation, from which the Christians of John's time should have been able to read off the symbolic meaning of most of the visions.

In this connection, I ought to mention that the term "God's people", as used in this work, will mean "Israel" in the context of the Old Testament and "the faithful church" in the context of the New Testament. The New Testament treats them, so I treat them, as one continuous history. That s why Christians felt entitled to appropriate for themselves the promises (and warnings) of the Old Testament.

Therefore, my own approach to understanding the book of Revelation will work by re-creating what they must have been doing instinctively. At every step, I will be looking for echoes from the books of the Old

Testament, A detailed index of the allusions which have been discovered, book by book, will be found at the end of the work.

While we're on the subject of symbolic interpretation, something should be said about the symbolism of number. A select group of numbers have significance in this book:

*3* Given the Christian setting, we should not be surprised to find triads in Revelation. There is the implied Trinity, of course, together with allusions to the past-present-future division of time, and also a running theme of "heavens, earth and sea" as the basic structure of the world.

*4* Based on the four main compass points, the general sense of this number is "in all directions" or "from all directions", or "covering everything".

*7* The number of Creation, because of the "Creation week" account in Genesis, and consequently the number associated with the Creator God. A small group of significant numbers have been derived from that connection. Thus;

*6* Associated with humanity, because humanity was made on the sixth day of the Creation week.

*8* Associated with Christ, because he was raised from the dead (in the thinking of the early church) on "the eighth day of the week", the day following the seventh. So the day of his Resurrection could be seen as an eighth day of Creation, completing and perfecting the process.

And the time when the Beast troubles the church will be identified as a period of *half of seven*- that is, half the time which God has assigned him.

*10* I see this as the number of completeness, or "the whole world".

*1000* An intensified version of 10.

Elsewhere in scripture and tradition, the multiplication of 7 and 10 gives rise to *70*, which has the implied meaning "the completeness of God's plan" or "what God does for the whole world".

*12* The number associated with God's people, because of the twelve tribes of Israel.

*144,000* Another multiplied number, combining the intensified version of 10 with an intensified version of 12.

A word of warning, prompted partly by that last number. I take the Bible seriously, but taking scripture seriously is not always quite the same thing as taking it literally (" ...to send out labourers into the harvest..."). How shall I put it? Revelation is a book crammed with symbols. As I work through the visions, I may find symbolic meaning *instead of* literal meaning in more places than some people will be expecting. However, I'm writing in faith and in good faith, and look for a better understanding of the message which God wants his people to hear.

Quotations in this discussion will normally come from the Revised Standard Version (RSV), and other translations will be identified when they appear. Since I am not an American, the famous translation published in 1611 will be identified as the Authorized Version (AV).

On those few occasions when Latin words are used, or when words are quoted from the Greek text, they will appear in the Roman alphabet, capitalized. I have two good reasons for not using Greek lettering. In the first place, it seems desirable, for the reading comfort of those who don't know Greek, that they should at least be able to vocalise the words which they see in front of them. In the second place, to be honest, I never did get around to discovering how to make my keyboards deliver Greek lettering to the page. So my practice has the double advantage of virtue and necessity.

# 1

# FEAR NOT

## (Revelation Chapter 1)

V1 "The revelation of Jesus Christ… to show to his servants what must soon take place."

This introductory chapter must be understood against the background of the troubled state of the church, implied in v9 by "tribulation and patient endurance" and by John's apparent exile in Patmos. So the first key point in the message is that the events to be described in this book are events which must happen and which must happen soon. The rescue mission cannot be prevented or delayed.

What is the definition of "soon"? I take it to be about the speed of God's response to the relevant crisis. The first crisis of the Roman church ended with Nero, but the endemic hostility came to an end only after a period of something less than three hundred years. The crisis of the church under the Beast has not yet begun (at the time of writing), but the elasticity of "soon" is one of the reasons why we will need patience and endurance.

John validates the message of hope by spelling out where it comes from. It was God who gave the revelation to Jesus Christ. Christ then sent his angel (that is, the representative seen later in the chapter) to "his servant John". John saw the vision and gives his testimony about the vision, and the blessing extends the line of transmission to those who read the words aloud and those who hear and absorb them.

V4 "Grace to you and peace."

This prayer, though a standard greeting in all Paul's letters, is not just a polite formula. It contains a condensed theology. To summarise more briefly than it deserves, "grace" is the freely-given act of God in Christ that deals with our sin, and our "peace" follows on from the fact that our sin has been dealt with. Paul says "We have peace with God through our Lord Jesus Christ", through whom "we have obtained access to the grace in which we stand" (Romans ch5 vv1-2). Here is our first reminder that the work of Christ in saving us from sin is at the root of his power to save us from human oppression.

In Paul's letters, the grace and peace are offered "from God our Father and from the Lord Jesus Christ". In this passage, they come from a three-fold source.

*"From him who was and is and is to come".*

The probable meaning of God's Hebrew name is "He who lives" or "He who is". This expanded version looks like the natural consequence of thinking in Greek, which is more interested than Hebrew in expressing the past-present-future aspect of time. The Lord God adds, in v8, that he is the Almighty and also the "Alpha and Omega", the first and last letters of the Greek alphabet. So in two different ways the all-embracing present is extended into past and future. In short, the Eternal One.

*"From the seven spirits which are before the throne."*

But the number "seven", in Revelation, is almost a label meaning "belonging to God". So here is the seven-fold Spirit, or the Spirit belonging to God. That is, the Holy Spirit.

V5 "From Jesus Christ."
Christ himself is then described in three different ways;

*"Faithful witness."*

This name comes, ultimately, from the Cross. In the "court-scene" imagery found in John's writings, Christ is our "advocate with the Father" (1 John ch2 v1). This makes him our faithful witness against the hostile testimony of Satan, who appears in this book as "the accuser of the brethren". The scene is one of the images of our redemption, holding the promise that our sins will not be held against us.

*"First-born of the dead."*

This name comes, of course, from the Resurrection. "First-born", because he's to be followed by many others. So this holds the promise of our own resurrection from the dead.

*"Ruler of kings on earth."*

This name comes, ultimately, from the Ascension, with which we associate the fact that he is to be called "Lord", the name at which "every knee shall bow"(Philippians ch2 v10). So, as a name, it holds the promise that the oppression of the "kings of earth" can be overruled.

In these three different ways, from the Eternal One, from the Spirit, and from Jesus Christ, the grace and peace come to us from a source of power. But John hasn't finished explaining what Christ does for us.

We benefit from what was.

*"To him who loves us and has freed us from our sins by his blood"*

That is, by his death on the Cross. In other words, he's already won a victory for us and won us freedom from oppression in the area that matters most.

*What is.*
*"...and made us a kingdom, priests to his God and Father."*

This echoes what the Israelites were told after the Exodus; "You shall be to me a kingdom of priests, a holy nation" (Exodus ch19 v6). In other words, the church are now God's people Israel, or at least an extension of God's people. Glory and dominion belong to him, because of these things which he has done.

*What is to come.*

V7 "Behold, he is coming with clouds and every eye will see him, every one who pierced him; and all the tribes of the earth will wail on account of him."

This combines themes from two of the prophets. One prophet sees "one like a son of man" who is coming "with the clouds of heaven" to be presented with dominion over the nations of the earth (Daniel ch7 vv13-

14). Another foresees that the families of Israel will see and mourn over "the one whom they had pierced" (Zechariah ch12 v10).

Matthew brings the two themes together and extends them to the tribes of the earth at large, who will mourn when they see the coming of the Son of man. In the same gospel, Jesus identifies himself as the Son of man. So John here combines the two themes in the same way that Matthew does, while spelling out more clearly the fact that the mourners will be the ones who pierced him. In other words, his coming in glory implies the defeat of his enemies and ours.

V10 "I was in the Spirit on the Lord's day."

After that general introduction, the beginning of the visions themselves. A day which began as a celebration of the Resurrection of Christ is a very appropriate setting for a message about the benefits of Resurrection power. For that reason, I shall ignore the revisionist theory that he was meditating on that Old Testament expectation "the Day of the Lord". John hears a voice behind him, and when he turns round he sees the angel (the visible representative of Christ) promised in the first verse.

V12 "I saw seven golden lampstands."

These will be identified as the seven churches listed in v11 (or the seven-fold church, the church of God)..There's another layer of meaning which can be found, when we follow the connecting links elsewhere in scripture. Firstly, the seven lampstands are identified as "the eyes of the Lord which range through the whole earth" (Zechariah ch4 v10). But here in Revelation (ch5 v6) the same seven eyes are identified with the seven-fold Spirit already mentioned in v4. So the seven lampstands are also an indicator of the presence of the Holy Spirit in the church.

John sees the figure of (the angel of) Christ, standing at the very centre of his community. We should recognise two visions of Daniel in the background of this description. One is the vision where we see God seated as "the Ancient of Days", and "one like a son of man" comes before him to receive dominion (Daniel ch7 v9).. The other is the great figure encountered by the prophet in Daniel ch10, clothed in linen and "a golden girdle", with "eyes like flaming torches", limbs of "burnished bronze", and a voice "like the sound of a multitude" (Daniel ch10 vv5-6). He proceeds to warn us about a forthcoming hostile ruler, who will "exalt himself and magnify himself above every god" (Daniel ch11 v36).

V13 "One like a son of man."

As already mentioned, this phrase identifies the figure who appears before the Ancient of Days.

V14 "His head and hair were white as white wool, white as snow."

However, this detail belongs to the Ancient of Days himself, representing God on his throne. The visual distinction between the two figures has been blurred a little.

Apart from "sound of many waters", which has been borrowed from Ezekiel's encounter with God (Ezekiel ch1 v24), most of the other details are drawn from the vision of Daniel ch10. The implication is that we must expect the rest of the book to contain another account of a hostile ruler setting himself against God.

V16 "From his mouth issued a sharp two-edged sword."

This points us towards the power of the Word, which is "sharper than a two-edged sword" to discern the intentions of the heart (Hebrews ch4 v12). At the same time, we should not forget the words of the Servant in Isaiah- "He has made my mouth like a sharp sword" (Isaiah ch49 v2). While the Branch of Jesse would be able to "smite the earth with the rod of his mouth" (Isaiah ch11 v4). Both passages are about the power of the Word in dealing with the wicked and restoring God's people in righteousness. Of course we understand both the Servant and the Branch as referring to Jesus himself.

*"His face was like the sun shining in full strength."*

In Malachi, the coming of the Lord's "day" would have a double effect. It would be "burning like an oven" against the arrogant and evildoers. But for those who fear the name of the Lord, the sun of righteousness would be rising "with healing in its wings" (Malachi ch4 vv1-2).

So all these visual details are presenting the message that the person at the centre of the church has the power to restore his people by overcoming the power of the oppressor.

V17 "He laid his right hand upon me, saying 'Fear not.'"
John had fallen at his feet "as though dead". The prostration of the prophet and the uplifting response are both echoes of Daniel ch10 and Ezekiel ch1 The more obvious and immediate meaning is "Don't be afraid of me". But the deeper and more important meaning is "Your community must not be afraid of anything else." This assurance depends on our knowing who the speaker is and what he can do.

*"Fear not, I am the first and the last and the living one."*
This echoes words found in Isaiah; "Fear not, O Jacob my servant… I am the first and the last, besides me there is no God (Isaiah ch44 vv2-6). We may also compare it with what God says about himself earlier in the chapter. "First and last" corresponds with "Alpha and Omega"; "the living one" echoes the frequently used title "the living God"; and the full combination adds up to the equivalent of "who is and who was and who is to come".

V18 "I died, and behold I am alive for evermore."
But this figure who has just been quoting what God says about himself now identifies himself more clearly as Jesus Christ, who was raised from the dead. As the resurrected one, he holds "the keys of death and Hades", which is presumably about his ability to unlock the doors of death and let people out. It is the promise of resurrection life for the rest of us.
So the key message of this chapter, and indeed the central message of Revelation as a whole, is this:

*"I have the power of God, the Resurrection power.*
So do not fear the power of sin.
Do not fear the power of oppression.
Do not fear the events which "must take place" in order to overcome the power of oppression.Fear not.

# 2

# WARNINGS AND PROMISES

## (Revelation Chapters 2&3)

These letters are to be received by seven great churches of the Roman province of Asia, on the western coast of what is now Turkey. They are being sent in the name of the Christ who showed himself to John in the first chapter. Each time he introduces himself by referring to one of the details in that vision, but I don't think there's much to be gained from trying to match the details to the individual churches.

On the face of it, each letter is addressed to the "angel" of the relevant church. Yet the contents of the letters are clearly meant for the attention of the whole church membership- as in "some of you [plural] will be put in prison" (ch2 v10). I've already quoted one example of God addressing his entire people under the name "Jacob". In modern times, we are able to treat "John Bull" and "Uncle Sam" as representative symbols of their communities, and even write to them in journalistic letters, and there is no reason why we should not treat "the angel of the church of Ephesus" in the same way. Christ is really speaking to the local church as a community.

Then he addresses each church according to their circumstances. Presumably they would have been relevant in the first instance to the named churches of John's own time, who should have been able to recognise themselves in the descriptions and apply the advice accordingly. Ministers with oversight of congregations like to use them to preach on the theme "Which one do we most resemble?"- a series of seven sermons, inevitably finishing with the conveniently ambiguous verdict of Laodicea.

But Revelation is a book written for the benefit of a church under persecution. So these letters can be applied most usefully by a church in similar circumstances, facing a general persecution combined with the temptations of other religions. Different parts of the church would be responding to the troubles with different degrees of success. It would then be possible for them to look into the letters and apply to themselves whatever words of rebuke or encouragement would be most appropriate for the way they were dealing with the crisis.

There are two sets of warnings in these letters (about the external danger and the internal danger), and one set of promises. I propose to treat these themes in turn.

### The threat of oppression

"I know where you dwell, where Satan's throne is" (ch2 v13)

Before we do anything else, we need to understand the place of Satan in Revelation. We must put aside many of the associations which have attached themselves to that name, such as "temptation" and "control of the occult". What matters here is that Satan is the Accuser, as we discover in ch12. His basic function is to accuse the sins of men before God.

When he cannot accuse the sins of Christians, because of the Atonement, he gets his revenge by accusing them before the Imperial authorities. So the secondary function, which dominates this book, is that he is the grand promoter of the persecution of Christians. This connection is reaffirmed later in the same verse, by the statement that "Antipas my witness... was killed among you where Satan dwells".

We must bear that in mind as we try to identify "Satan's throne." Many candidates have been suggested. Pergamum was a former capital with a collection of well-known temples. One popular candidate has been the temple of Zeus, as the "high God" of Greek culture, and the most direct public rival to the Biblical Creator God. Another option is to draw attention to the serpent-form associated with the healing god Aesculapius, remembering that Satan is later labelled as "the great serpent" or "the dragon". In fact if Satan is understood as a promoter of non-Biblical religion, then the entire temple complex in the city could be seen as a massive power-base for his work.

But if Satan's business in Revelation is promoting persecution through the Imperial authorities, it would make sense that "Satan's throne" should be a reference to Imperial authority, and in particular to the Imperial cult.

So if we have to pinpoint any specific location within Pergamum (as distinct from the authority structure itself), I'm inclined to put my money on the temple dedicated to Rome – DEA ROMA- and to Augustus in 29 B.C.

*"The synagogue of Satan" (ch2 v9, ch3 v9)*

This, too, must be connected with the persecution of the church. In the Smyrna letter, which contains the first reference, the comment about "the slander of the Jews" is placed in the immediate context of "your tribulation" and "what you are about to suffer", and the fact that "the devil is about to throw some of you in prison." It would seem that the authorities were taking action against Christians on information received (DELATIO, in Roman legal parlance), and that some of this information was coming from the Jews.

The Jews would have been well-placed for this. The Jewish community was an established "licensed" religion (RELIGIO LICITA), while the Christian faith was not. In the early days of the church, when the church was only just separating out of the Jewish nation, the distinction would not have been clear-cut. Roman officials might have been slow to notice that a new group was emerging. Hostile Jews could have made it their business to explain the difference, and to draw the attention of the authorities to Christian meetings.

To illustrate the point, here is a complaint which comes from the following century; "For other nations have not inflicted on us and on Christ this wrong to such an extent as you have, who in very deed are the authors of the wicked prejudice against the Just One and us who hold by Him...you selected and sent out from Jerusalem chosen men through all the land to tell that the godless heresy of the Christians had sprung up, and to publish those things which all they who know us not speak against us. So that you are the cause not only of your own unrighteousness, but in fact that of all other men." "Dialogue with Trypho", ch17. Justin Martyr

*"Who say that they are Jews, but are not"* (ch2 v9, ch3 v9)

When Paul, in Acts, was visiting synagogues, he was able to speak to "Greeks" there as well as to Jews. There must have been a large number of "interested" Gentiles, potential proselytes, floating around the synagogue community. It seems likely that Paul was able to divert many of them to Christianity. But there may have been many others who ignored this distraction and attached themselves to the Jews instead, going on to make a full commitment. I see the possibility that the proverbial "zeal of the convert" then prompted them to take the lead and become the driving force in hostility to those among their fellow-Gentiles who took the Christian route. That would be one way to account for this enigmatic charge.

The menace which comes from external authority is a recurring theme in the Bible as a whole. The classic example in the Old Testament is the oppression suffered by the Israelites at the hands of the Egyptians, in which time Moses was raised up as God's champion for his people. The rule of the Beast will be an obvious variant of this theme. There might also be a future parallel to "the slanders of the Jews"; the faithful church would need to be wary of possible betrayal by former co-religionists willing to compromise with the authorities.

How should faithful believers be conducting themselves in the face of these dangers? There is clear advice which centres upon the words "patience" and "endurance". The churches are praised because "you have kept my word and have not denied my name" (ch3 v8), because "you held fast my name and you did not deny my faith" (ch2 v13). The key instruction, perhaps, which makes the endurance possible, is once again "Do not fear" (ch2 v10). These chapters are written to warn the churches, but also to give them an assurance that the promises offered at the end of the letters are available to "those who conquer."

*The threat of infidelity*
Christians also need to be wary of dangers within their own community. For example, there are "those who call themselves apostles but are not" (ch2 v2). These are presumably exploiting the tradition, going back to Paul's time, of giving hospitality to wandering Christian workers. They would be false apostles if not genuinely "sent" by anyone except themselves, and I think we can take it that their teaching would be unreliable as well.

And we're given the names of other local groups. The churches are warned against "the teaching of Balaam", the leadership of a "Jezebel", and the work and teachings of the "Nicolaitans".

The name of Balaam is associated with the events at Shittim; "The people began to play the harlot with the daughters of Moab. These invited the people to the sacrifices of their gods, and the people ate, and bowed down to their gods. So Israel yoked himself to Baal of Peor". (Numbers ch25 vv1-3) The most significant point here is the combination of two attractions, the attraction of immorality leading the people on to other gods. The comment in the letter to Pergamum seems to be describing a more topical version of the same combination, when it says that Balaam was the one who "taught Balak to put a stumbling-block before the sons of Israel, that they might eat food sacrificed to idols and practice immorality". (ch2 v14).

Then there is the prophetess "Jezebel". The original Jezebel was promoting idolatry, in the form of the Tyrian version of Baal. Her only known association with immorality comes from Jehu's angry response; "What peace can there be as long as the harlotries and the sorceries of your mother Jezebel are so many?" (2 Kings ch9 v22) But the teaching of the Revelation version is explained in exactly the same terms as the teaching of Balaam. She beguiles the servants of God to "practise immorality and to eat food sacrificed to idols". (ch2 v20)

When Paul's advising the church in Corinth, a few decades previously, he's troubled by the same combination. He makes a very pointed reference to the affair at Shittim (as well as the story of the golden calf); "Do not be idolaters, as some of them were, as it is written, 'The people sat down to eat and drink and rose up to dance'. We must not indulge in immorality, as some of them did, and twenty-three thousand fell in a single day". (1 Cor. ch10 vv8-9)

He's also obliged, very specifically, in the same chapter, to address the problem of "meat sacrificed to idols". His real objection is to meat which is *being* sacrificed to idols at the time of eating. That is to say, he does not want his followers to be taking part in the sacrificial meals of other cults (which is precisely what was happening in Numbers). "What pagans sacrifice, they sacrifice to demons and not to God. I do not want you to be partners with demons". ( 1 Cor. ch10 v20) Presumably this is the real point of the objection in the Revelation letters.

And what about the Nicolaitans? We're told nothing about them, except that Jesus hates them. The name appears to derive from the words NIKOS ("victory") and LAOS ("people"). One theory is that John calls them this because they're acting "against God's people". But my reading of the situation is that this is a name which the group have chosen for themselves In which case, surely, the intended meaning would have been something more self-approving?

Perhaps we can find clues again in the letter to Corinth. Paul quotes and criticises comments made by his correspondents, like "All of us possess knowledge" (1 Cor ch8 v1) and "All things are lawful for me" (1 Cor. ch6 v12). Commentators think they can see an air of smugness and complacency in those remarks, a sense that people with superior knowledge can afford to ignore conventional restraints. They suggest that this attitude might be partly responsible for a self-indulgent willingness to compromise with immorality and idolatry.

Much would be explained if the people being criticised in these two chapters were developing the same kind of attitude. It would explain why the followers of "Balaam" and "Jezebel" were as lax as some of the Corinthians. It would explain why the followers of "Jezebel" were calling their philosophy "the deep things"; "the deep things of Satan", according to John, but perhaps "the deep things of God" in their own usage. (ch2 v24) And it would account for the triumphalist overtones of the nickname of the Nicolaitans- "We are the people of victory!"

What's emerging from these reflections is the sense that the integrity of the faith was under threat from within the community, from people feeling the attraction of other forms of religion, and attempting to compromise. This is another recurring theme in the Bible as a whole. The classic example, in the Old Testament, is the attraction of the god Baal, in which time Elijah was raised up as God's champion for his people.

The rest of Revelation has very little to say on the subject, apart from vague references to the "harlotry" and "sorceries" of Babylon. We can hardly doubt, though, from past experience, that the integrity of the faith would be under threat once more, under hostile conditions. There would be "false apostles", sending themselves in their own financial interests, more interested in exercising control than in offering reliable teaching. There would be parallels to "sharing meals with idols", in the sense that Christians would be drawn to the beliefs and practices of other religions, and attempting to import them into Christian life.

How should faithful Christians be conducting themselves in the face of these dangers? There is very clear advice, which can be summed up in the instruction "Hold fast what you have" (ch3 v11), meaning the true teaching of Christ. They also have instructions about the false teaching they encounter. They are to "test" it (ch2 v2)- considering, perhaps, amongst other things, what it says about the reality of Christ and the reality of what happened on the Cross. They are "not to tolerate" it (ch2 v20), meaning they should not allow it to be taught within the church. They are "not to hold " it (ch2 v34)- if it cannot be escaped, it can at least be ignored. And finally, they are "not to take part" (ch2 v14)- they should not try to compromise the Christian faith by combining it with other religions.

It is worth repeating; these chapters are written to warn the churches, but also to give them an assurance that the promises offered at the end of the letters are available to "those who conquer." Let us, then, look at the promises themselves.

*The promise*
Each of these letters concludes with a promise given by Christ to those who are able to "conquer" the difficulties.

EPHESUS
"To him I will give to eat of the tree of Life" (ch2 v7)
The theme of the tree of Life is familiar from Genesis. The tree was planted at the centre of the Garden, and Adam and Eve were not forbidden to eat from it. The obvious implication is that they did eat from it, on a regular basis, until they fell into sin. They were then removed from the Garden with the express purpose that they should not [continue to] eat its fruit. So they were denied access to Life and became subject to death- they were demoted, as it were, from "Life" to "life". Then the promise of the

fruit of the tree (which is fulfilled in ch22) is an offer to restore what was lost to them by sin.

### SMYRNA

"He shall not be hurt by the second death" (ch2 v11)

The explanation is given in ch20 that the "second death" is experienced by those whose names are not written in the "Book of Life". That is to say, they don't qualify to enjoy the new Jerusalem, Life in the presence of God, described in the following chapters. So clearly not being hurt by "the second death" means becoming part of the new city.

### PERGAMUM

"To him I will give to eat of the hidden manna... "I will give him a white stone, with a new name written on the stone" (ch2 v17)

The original manna was the food God gave to the Israelites in the wilderness. But this manna, as Jesus pointed out, was not "the true bread from heaven". "Your fathers ate the manna in the wilderness and they died... I am the living bread which comes down from heaven; if anyone eats of this bread, he will live for ever." (John ch6 49-51) The "hidden" (or spiritual) manna is clearly meant to indicate that same "bread from heaven". So this is another version of the promise of the tree of Life, relating it to the Life which comes direct from Christ.

The "white stone" has been interpreted in a number of ways. I think the interpretation which best fits the developing theme of these promises is that it signifies the absence of guilt. One explanation sometimes offered is that a white stone was used in trials to indicate a "not guilty verdict". Alternatively- and not for the last time in Revelation- there may be a reference to Zechariah's vision about the High Priest Joshua; "Upon the stone which I have set before Joshua...I will engrave its inscription, says the Lord of hosts, and I will remove the guilt of this land in a single day" (Zechariah ch3 v9). Whatever that white stone represents (commentators disagree), the significance is clearly the removal of guilt.

The "new name" is also about freedom from sin. Having a "new name" means having a new identity, a new kind of character. More than once, in the prophets, God tells his people that he will give them a new name after the relationship has been healed. He has known them as "Not-pitied" or "Not-my-people" (Hosea ch1 vv8-9), and he has known them as "Forsaken" or "Desolate" (Isaiah ch62 v4), but he promises to give them different names. The new names he offers, like "Hephzibah" ("my delight-is-in-her") and "Beulah" ("married") are the symbol of forgiveness and reconciliation. The new, spiritual, name mentioned here would have the same significance.

So the white stone with the new name indicates freedom from sin. But sin was the obstacle which prevented access to the tree of Life. Then the combined promises made to the church in Pergamum are once more the equivalent of the promise of Life.

THYATIRA

"I will give him power over the nations; and he shall rule them with a rod of iron...I will give him the morning star" (ch2 vv26-28)

These things are part of the description of the glory that belongs to Christ himself. The Lord says to "my son" in the Psalms; "You shall break them with a rod of iron, and dash them in pieces like a potter's vessel" (Psalm 2 v9). And this is quoted as the destiny of the "male child" born in Revelation ch12 v5. While "the morning star" is a title which Christ claims for himself in ch22 v16. So receiving these things means being closely identified with Christ. It means belonging to Christ, being part of him- even "ruling" together with him. And the consequence of belonging to Christ is freedom from sin; "There is therefore now no condemnation for those who are in Christ"- Romans ch8 v1

Then belonging to Christ means freedom from sin, and freedom from sin, as already observed, implies renewed access to the tree of Life.

SARDIS

"He shall be clad in white garments… I will not blot out his name from the Book of Life… I will confess his name before my Father" (ch3 v5)

These are alternative ways of describing the promises we've already seen. When Jesus is "confessing" his followers before his father, that means he is claiming them as his own; "So everyone who acknowledges me before men, I also will acknowledge before my father who is in heaven" (Matthew ch10 v32). But belonging to Christ is the precondition for freedom from sin.

Being clad in white garments, like having a new name, is the symbol of that new freedom from sin. Just as the filthy garments were taken away from the High Priest Joshua, in the Zechariah vision already mentioned, and replaced by clean ones. Similarly, white robes are given to the saints in heaven in the later chapters of Revelation. But freedom from sin, as already observed, is the precondition for access to Life. Finally, we know from the previous reference to ch20 that *not* being blotted out of the Book of Life is the same thing as *not* suffering the "second death". It means entering a new Life in the new Jerusalem.

### PHILADELPHIA

"I will make him a pillar in the Temple... I will write on him the name of God and the name of the city of my God...and my own new name" (ch3 v12).

The meaning of "pillar" is fully explained by the following phrase-"never shall he go out of it". A pillar is a permanent fixture. This is someone who will never leave the presence of God. To have the "name" of someone is to be closely identified with them, to belong to them. So to have the name of God means to belong to God. The "city of God" is the new Jerusalem described at the end of Revelation, representing God's people and the place where they dwell. So to have the name of that city means to belong to God's people. And to have the name of Christ means to belong to Christ.

All these things belong together, follow on from one another. He who conquers remains in the presence of God because he belongs to God. He belongs to God because he belongs to God's people. And he belongs to God's people because he belongs to Christ. That is the key to his permanent presence in the Temple.

### LAODICEA

"I will grant him to sit with me on my throne, as I myself conquered and sat down with my Father on his throne" (ch3 v21)

In other words, Christ carries him into the presence of the Father, so that he might live (and reign) in the company of both of them. This is the summary and completion of everything said in the previous promises. And, of course, the implication is eternal Life in the presence of God.

Thus the promise of Life has been given to every church in these two chapters. This is the promise which is fulfilled in the final chapters of Revelation.

*Stephen Disraeli*

# 3

# THE THRONE OF GOD

## (Revelation Chapter 4)

John is now called up ("in the Spirit") to the place of God's throne, where God "looks down from heaven and sees all the sons of men" (Psalm 33 vv13-14).. We should recognise three different encounters with God in the background of this scene. One is the meeting arranged for the "seventy elders of Israel" at Sinai (Exodus ch24 vv9-11). This event is associated with the Covenant between God and his people, as the sequel of the Covenant-sacrifice carried out by Moses. Another is Isaiah's vision in the Temple, which is associated with the sins of God's people and the promise that a remnant would be saved (Isaiah ch6 vv1-5) . But the most direct model is Ezekiel's vision by the river Chebar (Ezekiel ch1), associated with the oppression of God's people by the Babylonians.

V1 "Lo, in heaven an open door."
So Ezekiel saw the heavens "opened" before the Glory of the Lord came down to him.
"Come up hither, and I will show you what must take place after this."
He is being invited to see, from that standpoint, the events of the whole of the rest of Revelation.

V2 "A throne stood in heaven, with one seated on the throne."
Out of reverence, he does not name the ruler more exactly.

V3 "Round the throne was a rainbow."
This echoes the statement in Ezekiel; "Like the appearance of the bow that is in the cloud on the day of rain, so was the appearance of the

brightness round about" (Ezekiel ch1 v28). At the time of the Genesis flood, God promised not to flood the world again and offered the rainbow as a symbol of the promise. So this indicates the protective aspect of God. He is a God who sustains the world as well as ruling it.

V4 "Seated on the thrones were twenty-four elders, clad in white garments, with golden crowns upon their heads"

Here is another version of the "elders of Israel", the representatives of God's people in a close covenant relationship.. White garments are a symbol of redemption from sin. The thrones and crowns identify them as kings. As the people in John's time would have known, permission to sit in the king's presence is a great honour and privilege in itself, normally allowed only to other kings. "What is man that thou art mindful of him? Thou hast made him little less than God, and dost crown him with honour and glory" (Psalm 8 vv4-5).

I've already suggested an interpretation of the symbolic number "seventy", which applies to the elders at Sinai. For this vision, the number "twenty-four" is sometime taken as "twelve for Israel, twelve for the church". My difficulty with that theory is the Israel and the church, in my understanding of the Bible, are one single continuing community, rather than two communities. God's people could be covered by a single "twelve", as in ch12.

An alternative suggestion, which I like better, is to match the number with the twenty-four priestly families of the tribe of Levi (1 Chronicles ch24 v4). They are already identified as kings. If they are also to be identified as priests, that makes them a visual expression of their own song in the next chapter; "Thou didst redeem men for God, and hast made them a kingdom and priests to our God."

V5 "From the throne issue flashes of lightning, and voices and peals of thunder".

This is another echo of the Covenant-making at Sinai. They express God's intention to impose his will. This may become "wrath", but the wrath is already limited by the protective aspect of God implied by the rainbow, and also by the Covenant relationship implied by the presence of the elders.

"Seven torches of fire, which are the seven spirits of God,"

I stand by my previous explanation, that this is the seven-fold Spirit of God, or the Holy Spirit. All the way through the Bible, the Spirit of God is the expression of God's power, in one form or another.

V6 "A sea of glass, like crystal."

This is the firmament or sky, seen from above. Some "portable" version of this firmament is found in other encounters. When the elders at Sinai saw their God, "there was under his feet as it were a pavement of sapphire stone, like the very heaven for clearness". The moving throne in Ezekiel's vision was resting on "the likeness of a firmament, shining with crystal". But John has been caught up (in vision) to the real thing, to that place where God looks down upon the earth.

*"Round the throne, on each side of the throne, are four living creatures, full of eyes in front and behind."*

The four creatures are from Ezekiel's vision, though the eyes in that vision belong to the "wheels" which accompany them. Their location in the Greek text is "in the middle of the throne and round the throne". Translators prefer to rewrite or omit that puzzling first phrase. Perhaps the best solution is to see them, as in Ezekiel, in the middle of and moving around the space under the throne. In the first instance, they may have been meant to represent "the four winds", which would naturally emanate from and remain close to God's throne among the clouds.

V7 "Like a lion... like an ox... with the face of a man... like a flying eagle."

These come from Ezekiel (where each creature has all four faces). It's been observed that each of these four living things has a kind of supremacy in its own sphere. Thus the eagle can claim supremacy among the birds of the air, and it was "on eagles' wings" that God brought Israel out of Egypt (Exodus ch19 v4). The lion can claim supremacy amongst the wild beasts of the land, and "the lion of the tribe of Judah appears in the next chapter.

The ox can claim supremacy among domesticated animals, and "horns" are a symbol of power all the way through the Old Testament. While humanity, by God's decree, was given supremacy amongst all of them (Genesis ch1 v26). Perhaps, then, they represent the living world at large, in the same way that the elders represent God's people.

At the same time, we must not lose that sense of them as "the four winds", because the four winds have been associated with the judgements of God in more than one prophecy. God threatens to send "the four winds of heaven" to scatter Elam (Jeremiah ch49 v36). The four chariots of Zechariah ch6, with their attendant horses, are "sent forth to the four winds of heaven", with judgemental purpose. We'll be coming back to that theme later, when the holding back of "the four winds of the earth" in ch7 interrupts the judgements which were running through ch6, judgements which were summoned by these four living creatures.

V8 "Each of them with six wings"
This detail is borrowed from the seraphim in Isaiah's vision.

*"Holy, holy, holy, is the lord God Almighty, who was and is and is to come."*
The four creatures are praising God without ceasing. The first half of that line comes from the seraphim, the second half from the first chapter of this book. Thus they are focussing on what God is in himself. They are telling us that God is self-existent and eternal, and that he is "holy", distinct and separate from the universe.

Every time the four creatures give this praise (which is unceasing), the elders are offering their royal authority back to God. This is parodied later, in ch17, when the ten kings ae giving over their own authority to the Beast. Their own praise is focussed on God's action beyond himself; he deserves honour and glory because he created all, and because he did do by an act of conscious will.

I think there's value in summarising the difference between the God portrayed in this chapter and a pantheistic God.

This chapter teaches us that God is distinct from the universe (the message of the living creatures), that God brings into existence the universe (the message of the elders), and that he actively engages with the universe (the message of the rest of the imagery).

A pantheistic God would be identifiable with the universe. Therefore it would not be distinct from something which was not itself, it would not bring into existence something which was not itself, and it would not actively engage with something which was not itself.

The God of Revelation needs to be a Creator-God, somebody engaged in his Creation, because only such a God could carry through these events to their final conclusion. The God who finally says "Behold, I make all things new" could only be the God who brought them into existence in the first place.

*Stephen Disraeli*

# 4

# THE SCROLL

## (Revelation Chapter 5)

V1 "A scroll written within and on the back, sealed with seven seals".

This scroll appears, or has just been spotted, in the right hand of the one "seated on the throne". Its function is demonstrated in the next chapter, where we see the progressive opening of the scroll. The seals are broken one by one, and each time a seal is broken something happens. The implication is that the scroll contains the events of the next chapter- not the description of them, but the events themselves. Each time a seal is broken, the scroll is unrolled a little further. Each time the scroll is unrolled a little further, one more event is "released" into the world.

I think we have to imagine that the seals were fixed onto the scroll, stage by stage, as the scroll was being rolled up from the bottom (or the far end). The key point would be the location of the seal. On the edge of the parchment, I suggest, holding the rolled portion together like a paperclip, so that the scroll could not be unrolled beyond that point. The last of the seals would go on top, holding it all together. Then the seals would be broken in reverse order, with the effect that we see in the next chapter.

V3 "No one in heaven or on earth or under the earth was able to open the scroll or look into it"

One version of John's triple division of the created universe. Since God himself placed the seals (as we know, because there are seven of them), it's not surprising that nobody else can break them.

V4 "I wept much that no one was found worthy".

He weeps, because the contents of the scroll have unsurpassable importance. They include the events of ch6, which are God's response to the immediate persecution of the church, expressing his wrath against the oppressors. Then the seventh seal releases the rest of Revelation, all the way down to the new Jerusalem in the last chapters. In effect, all these things are locked up in the scroll, and they cannot happen before the scroll is opened.

V5 "The Lion of the tribe of Judah, the Root of David, has conquered." Obviously, this points us towards Jesus.

V6 "I saw a Lamb standing as though it had been slain."

In other words, he has conquered by means of the Cross ("slain") and the Resurrection ("standing"). The Lamb image identifies him with "the Lamb of God, who takes away the sin of the world" (John ch1 v29). John sees him standing among the elders, the representatives of his people.

Other visual details show that he has been endowed with seven horns (the seven-fold power of God), and with seven eyes (the seven-fold Spirit of God, the Holy Spirit).

V8 "And when he had taken the scroll, the four living creatures and the twenty-four elders fell down before the Lamb, each holding a harp, and with golden bowls full of incense, which are the prayers of the saints".

Sometimes it's better not to visualise all the details of Revelation. Otherwise we would be obliged to admire their dexterity in falling to their knees without spilling the bowls The prayers are brought in at this point because "the saints" (the faithful church) want the further acts of salvation which will be released when the scroll is opened.

V9 "Worthy art thou to take the scroll and to open its seals."

They call him "worthy"- AXIOS. The root of this word carries the sense, amongst other things, that something "has weight". This is not just about power, but about moral authority.

*"For thou wast slain and by thy blood didst ransom men for God."*

We know that the Lamb of God takes away the sin of the world, (John ch1 v29), but how does that give him any right to break the seals? The answer must be that "the sin of the world" is the reason why the seals are there. They represent the complex of sin-and-death which bars our way to Life in the presence of God.

By breaking the power of sin, the Lamb is able to bring us into the new Jerusalem with renewed access to the Tree of Life (ch22), and also, along the way, to break the power of human oppression. The destruction of the Beast is one of the by-products of the act of Atonement, which is the real driving-force behind the events of Revelation.

Something new and wonderful has happened in the history of Eternity. Hence the praise which follows, in which the living creatures and the elders are joined by "every creature in heaven and on earth and under the earth and in the sea. In short, there's an explosion of joy and praise beginning around the throne and spreading out to fill the totality of the universe.

*Stephen Disraeli*

# 5

# THE FOUR HORSEMEN

## (Revelation Chapter 6)

V1 "When the Lamb opened one of the seven seals, I heard one of the four living creatures say 'Come!'"

The traditional version is "Come and see!", but the text accepted in modern translations makes more sense. John is already on the spot and doesn't keep moving from one vantage point to another. Each call is a summons addressed to one of the four horsemen. The horsemen are the agents of the living creatures, who are themselves the agents of God. Since the living creatures may be seen as the four winds, the unleashing of the four horsemen here is another way of visualising the act of sending "four winds from the four quarters of heaven", as threatened in Jeremiah ch49 v36.

We should also recognise, in the background of this chapter, the four horses of Zechariah ch1 and the horses and chariots of Zechariah ch6. In fact we cannot understand John's message for the church of his time unless we first understand Zechariah's message to the Israel of his own time.

The most important point about the setting of Zechariah's book is the problem of "other nations". Judah had been invaded by the Assyrians in the past, they had been conquered by the Babylonians, and now they were living as part of the mighty Persian empire.

In the vision of the first chapter, the prophet is shown four differently-coloured horses, which have been out patrolling the earth. The report they bring back is that "the earth remains at rest" This prompts an outburst from the angel of the Lord, complaining about the contrasting state of Judah themselves. They are not "at rest" because they've been feeling the effects of the Lord's anger. The Lord responds with comforting words; he says that he is "jealous" on behalf of Jerusalem, and also "very angry with the nations that are at rest".

In the sixth chapter, we learn what he's going to do about it. A similar set of horses, with chariots, goes out on patrol again. The most important mission is to "the north country", the origin point of all the recent invaders. There seem to be at least two schools of thought about the translation of Zechariah ch6 v8; as between, say "brought my spirit to rest on the land of the north" (Jerusalem Bible), and "set my spirit at rest in the north country" (RSV). The first suggests that the north is feeling God's anger, the second suggests, perhaps, that God's spirit was previously troubled. I prefer the sense of the second version, because it implies a neat, logical reversal of the situation in the first chapter.

In the first chapter; Earth at rest, so God's people not at rest, therefore God's spirit not at rest. The achievement of the sixth chapter would then be; Earth's rest is overturned, the rest of God's people (implicitly) restored, and therefore the rest of God's spirit restored. God is expressing his jealousy for his people by expressing his anger against, taking action against, the oppressors of his people.

The four horses of this chapter of Revelation come in four different colours. I don't see any specific message in the colours, except "These horses are much the same horses that you saw operating in Zechariah, and you should be expecting them to have the same function". The parallel implies a similar setting for the events in Revelation. That is, the world at large- at least the portion of the world controlling God's people- would be "at rest". Indeed the "Roman peace" of the empire at large (outside the immediate vicinity of the Imperial palace) has become proverbial.

God's people themselves, in contrast, would not be "at rest". They would be oppressed and in trouble (partly as a result of their own former sins). God would then be "jealous" on behalf of his people, and "very angry with the nations that are at rest". These horsemen then come out into the world as an expression of that anger. This chapter should have been read by the church of John's time as a promise that God would respond to their troubles, and that he would take action against their oppressors.

In tradition, the horsemen are identified as "Pestilence, War, Famine and Death". This echoes Jeremiah's warning that the inhabitants of

Jerusalem would be divided between "pestilence, the sword, famine, and captivity" (Jeremiah ch15 v2). In Ezekiel's "four sore acts of judgement" on the land, captivity is replaced by "wild beasts" (Ezekiel ch14 v21, ch5 v17). I call this pattern of prophecy the "Four Fates". Let's take the four horsemen of this chapter, one by one.

V2 "Behold, a white horse, and its rider had a bow, and a crown was given to him, and he went out conquering and to conquer."

Yes, that's Pestilence. There's a tradition in ancient culture that plague comes from the arrows shot by the sun and the moon. It's reflected in one of the Psalms; "You will not fear the terror of the night, Nor the arrow that flies by day, Nor the pestilence that stalks in darkness, Nor the destruction that wastes at noonday." (Psalm 91 vv5-6). We get the same image at the beginning of Homer's Iliad, where the flying arrows of the angry god Apollo are wreaking havoc in the Greek camp. This horseman "goes out to conquer" as an epidemic or even as a pandemic.

Revisionist explanations do exist. One theory going back at least to Matthew Henry identifies him with the Christ-figure of ch19 (who carries a sword, not a bow), or as "the gospel". But if these four horsemen really are connected with the Four Fates and with the vengeful horses of the Zechariah visions, that rules out a benign interpretation of any one of them. "Conquest"? "Conflict"? But what, then, would be the difference between that and "taking peace from the earth", which is supposed to be the job of the next horseman? And in my understanding of the narrative in Revelation, it's much too early to expect the "coming of the Antichrist", which is another popular proposal. I'll need to enlarge on that point at a later time.

V4 "Another horse, bright red; its rider was permitted to take peace from the earth."

This might cover any kind of conflict, including civil wars and rioting. The "permission" comes implicitly from God.

V6 "A quart of wheat for a denarius and three quarts of barley for a denarius".

Setting very high prices, apparently, for the food items. Hence "Famine". Ironically, there is no shortage of luxury items like wine.

V8 A pale horse and its rider's name was Death, and Hades followed him; and they were given power over a fourth of the earth, to kill with sword and with famine and with pestilence and by wild beasts of the earth." In other words, they are accompanied by Ezekiel's version of the Four Fates.

One modern popular theory sees the four "horsemen" as four distinct events, coming at intervals. One objection to this view is that there is nothing outstanding, in human history, about these problems as individual events. In any case, there is also something odd about the fact that Death appears as the last horseman in the series and *only* as the last horseman. Pestilence, War and Famine are causes of death in their own right; yet if they came separately, they would be coming in the absence of Death, which would be absurd.

So I'm convinced that John's expecting us to see a completely different picture. These horsemen are coming in quick succession, and, once they get going, they're running *together*. The three causes of death fan out across the world, their paths crossing and criss-crossing, while "Death" itself follows on close behind them to pick up all the corpses. In other words, these are not meant to be four distinct disasters, but the different components of one major, devastating disaster. The Four Fates.

For me, as an old student of history, it's only too easy to imagine a possible "feedback" effect. That is, as these disasters are developing and merging, they might be helping to aggravate one another. For example, pestilence and war would disrupt the growing of food and the transportation of food, which would aggravate shortages. Shortages would aggravate the loss of peace, with fighting at all levels of society from local markets to international frontiers. Any epidemic which was drastic enough to break down social structures would also help to "take peace from the earth". Finally, any combination of death and social breakdown which left bodies lying around unburied would aggravate the problem of disease.

In the opening of the fifth and sixth seals, we see two sets of reactions to the Four Horsemen event.

V9 "I saw under the altar the souls of those who had been slain for the word of God."

The first reaction comes from the martyrs, whose preceding deaths are presumably the reason for God's wrathful response. In other words, they are the immediate cause of what's happening. They are now set apart from the main action and commenting, as it were, from the side-lines.

They must be at the foot of the altar, "under" it in the sense of people standing in front of a structure much larger than themselves. I've seen the bizarre suggestion that the altar is hollow and serving to protect them, but there's no evidence in the Old Testament for altars being anything less than solid.

V10 "How long, O Lord, before thou wilt judge and avenge our blood on those who dwell on the earth?"

This is the classic Old Testament theme that the blood of a martyred man calls to God for justice. That goes right back to God's encounter with Cain; "The voice of your brother's blood is crying to me from the ground" (Genesis ch4 v10). So where John says "I saw the souls of the martyrs", we ought to understand that as "the blood of the martyrs". This follows from the principle that "the life is in the blood" (Leviticus ch17 v11).

In other words, the gruesome image appears to be that the appeal is coming from their blood, as it flows down the side of the altar where they were "sacrificed" and gathers in pools at the bottom. "Under the altar" in yet another sense.

The wording of the appeal is borrowed from one of the Psalms, a Psalm prompted by the Babylonian destruction of Solomon's Temple;; "How long, O Lord?... Let the avenging of the outpoured blood of thy servants be known among the nations before our eyes" (Psalm79 v5, v10). But why are they asking for vengeance, when they can see that the vengeance is already happening? It seems that they welcome the event as the beginning of God's justice, but they are looking for the process to be carried through to completion. They will be satisfied when they see the full destruction of evil power on earth.

V11 "They were each given a white robe and told to rest a little longer."

The answer given is "Not yet." For the moment, they must be content with their own reward, the white robe indicating redemption from sin.

"Until the number of their brethren should be complete, who were to be killed as they themselves had been."

They are to be joined by a second batch of martyrs. Consequently, the process of justice will be interrupted, and completion will be delayed, in order to allow a little breathing-space. There will be a "time of truce", which we see in the next chapter. When we come to examine the Beast, I will suggest that the Beast makes his first appearance in the world in the time of truce. That his reputation and power are based, in fact, on leading the world into recovery from the disastrous episode of the Four Horsemen. That's one of my reasons for not accepting the Beast himself as one of the series.

V12 "When he opened the sixth seal... there was a great earthquake."

The events which occur after the opening of the next seal are echoes of events in Old Testament prophecy. For example, the great earthquake itself echoes the earthquake which defines the beginning of Amos. This is important, because the collected prophecies of Amos help to mark a change in the way God was dealing with his people.

In the past, he had been guiding them, through his prophets, with a mixture of rebuke and encouragement, as the need arose. But the newer "writing prophets" of Israel and Judah were symptoms of the fact that God's people were increasingly reluctant to listen, and needed more urgent warnings about the dangers of disobedience. The earthquake marks the beginning of a great theme of "judgement", which finally culminated in the fall of Jerusalem to the Babylonians.

So the message in this event is about the beginning of God's judgement upon the world.

We see events in the heavens. The sun darkens, the moon turns red, and the stars disappear from view "as the fig-tree sheds its winter fruit when shaken by a gale". The sky then vanishes "like a scroll that is rolled up". In physical terms, atmospheric pollution could be enough to produce these effects.

But all these things are echoes of the Old Testament. When "the Lord is enraged against all nations", then "all the host of heaven shall rot away and the skies roll up like a scroll. (Isaiah ch34 v4). Again, we are told that "the sun shall be turned to darkness and the moon to blood" in the time before "the great and terrible day of the Lord" (Joel ch2 v31). The "day of the Lord" is the time when God is expected to come in power to impose his will upon the world and put things right. It is a terrible day, a time of judgement, for all those who are part of what needs to be put right.

So the message in these events is about the imminence of God's judgement upon the world.

V15 "They hid in the caves and among the rocks of the mountains."

The human response to these events brings in another set of echoes. This reaction is the equivalent of "Enter into the rock and hide in the dust from before the terror of the Lord" (Isaiah ch2 v10). That is a day when the pride of men will be humbled. In Jeremiah, the mountains are quaking and the hills move to and fro, while the heavens turn black, causing whole cities to take flight and "climb among rocks" (Jeremiah ch4 vv24-29).

V16 "Calling to the mountains and rocks, 'Fall on us and hide us'."

This is the expected plea of the people of Samaria (Hosea ch10 v8).

V17 "The great day of their wrath has come, who can stand before it?"

As in "For the Day of the Lord is great and terrible, who can endure it?" (Joel ch2 v11). "They", in this case, are the one seated on the throne and the Lamb, working together. So the message in all these reactions is that the peoples of the earth are recognising the coming of God's judgement.

In fact we should see this as the world's reaction to the episode of the Four Horsemen, the other side of the coin to the reaction of the martyrs. Indeed the fifth and sixth seals are one of the contrasting pairs that we find in Revelation. On the one hand, the martyrs can see God's work in these events and welcome it. On the other hand, the people of the world at large see the same work and are terrified. These are the two different ways of receiving the judgment of God.

The overtones of this chapter are a little ambivalent about the relation between God's people and God's judgement. One of the running themes of the Old Testament is that God's people suffer at the hands of outsiders because their own sins have prompted him to withdraw his protection. The classic explanation is in Judges; "And the people of Israel did what was evil in the sight of the Lord... So the anger of the Lord was kindled against Israel.. and he sold them into the power of their enemies round about" (Judges ch2 vv11-14).

This was the explanation of the fall of Samaria to the Assyrians-"because the people of Israel had sinned against the Lord their God" (2 Kings ch17 v7). And for the fall of Jerusalem to the Babylonians; "Because the people have forsaken me and polluted this place... I will cause their people to fall by the sword before their enemies" (Jeremiah ch4 vv4-7).

It may be suggestive, then, that some of the images in this chapter have been taken from God's warnings towards his own people. For example, the earthquake from Amos ch1, the darkened heavens from Joel ch2, and the mountain-shaking of Jeremiah ch4. Indeed the Four Fates, which are part of the structure of this chapter, were originally put forward as the destiny of Jerusalem. What do we make of this?

Of course the answer may be simply that these images were available as images of God's judgement, touching equally the world in general. But perhaps we should see a hint that the sufferings of the church had in a sense been "earned". The martyrs lost their lives partly because God withdrew his protection from the church, because of their idolatry and unfaithfulness and other sins. This could even apply to the church of John's time, and could certainly apply to any future church. In the pattern of the Old Testament, the chastisement of his people is frequently followed, as here, by vengeance on the enthusiastic agents of chastisement.

In my understanding of Revelation, as I've said, John is offering two messages of hope and encouragement. The first message is for the suffering church of his own time, the second for a future suffering church. What is this chapter describing, with respect to the first message? Some people would apply it to the "year of the four emperors" (A.D. 69), the political turmoil in Italy following the death of Nero. Others, to the reconquest of Judaea by Tito, culminating in the destruction of the Temple (A.D. 70). At least this might account for the "chastisement of God's people" overtones.

I have a third proposal, though it does require that the chapter be treated as genuine prophecy, rather than disguised history. There's an even better match for these events in the disastrous third century of the Roman Empire, covered by the Cambridge Ancient History under the title "The Imperial Crisis and Recovery" . It was a period of barbarian invasions, political turmoil, and economic turmoil, including at one stage "a widespread temporary crisis in production, connected with an excessive cultivation of the vine and a deficient cultivation of corn" (p238). There were also outbreaks of pestilence, including "that fearful plague that raged from Gallus to the death of Claudius" (p227).

In the words of Gibbon; "But a long and general famine was a calamity of a more serious kind. It was the inevitable consequence of rapine and oppression, which extirpated the produce of the present, and the hope of future harvests. Famine is almost always followed by epidemical diseases, the effect of scanty and unwholesome food... During some time, five thousand persons died daily in Rome, and many towns, that had escaped the hands of the barbarians, were entirely depopulated." Extrapolating from the records of corn distribution in Alexandria, Gibbon concludes that "war, pestilence and famine had consumed, in a few years, the moiety of the human species [in the Roman Empire]." ("Decline and Fall", ch11)

The Emperor Diocletian (A.D. 284-305) led the Empire into recovery and restructured the system of government. As part of his reforms, he then deemed it necessary to launch the most aggressive and most nearly universal campaign of Christian persecution that the church has ever known. To my mind, that qualifies Diocletian to be identified as the Beast, as regards the first of John's two messages.

*Stephen Disraeli*

# 6

# THE TIME OF TRUCE

## (Revelation Chapter 7)

V1 "I saw four angels standing at the four corners of the earth, holding back the four winds of the earth".

The previous chapter of this book covered a time of havoc. This chapter introduces a time of truce. The Four Horsemen had been summoned by the four Living Creatures, who may themselves originate from "the four winds" notionally supporting the throne of God in heaven. Holding back the four destructive winds means the suspension of the work of judgement. The martyrs have already been warned that their final vindication will be delayed.

*"That no wind might blow on earth or sea or against any tree."*

The Horsemen had been acting on humanity directly, partly by damaging human relationships. In the next stage, the postponed stage, they would have moved on to the natural world. The truce ends in the next chapter, when the angels with trumpets go into action, and the business of hurting the earth and the sea and the trees can begin in earnest.

V2 "Then I saw another angel…Do not harm the earth or the sea or the trees."

Of course they are acting on that instruction already, just by being there. The fifth angel's real assignment is to tell us what's happening.

V3 "Till we have sealed the servants of God upon their foreheads."

Paul has told us how God seals his people; "In [Christ] you also, who have heard the word of truth, the gospel of salvation, and have believed in him, were sealed with the promised Holy Spirit, which is the guarantee of our inheritance" (Ephesians ch1 vv13-14). And again; "It is God who establishes us with you in Christ and has commissioned us; he has put his seal upon us and given us his Spirit in our hearts as a guarantee" (2 Corinthians ch1 vv21-22). There's no suggestion that the servants here are sealed in a single moment. It would be part of the continuing process of people hearing the gospel of forgiveness and putting their trust in Christ.

V4 "One hundred and forty-four thousand".

I've already drawn attention to the symbolic meaning of number. "10" has been described as the number of completeness of perfection. I think of it as pointing towards "the full extent of the world". "1000" is 10 in cubic form. I think of it as God's version of 10, the full extent of *God's* world. And all the way through the Bible, "12" is the number which points us towards God's people. Now each tribe on the following list is numbered as "12" multiplied by "1000", and the multiplication by 12 is repeated because there are twelve tribes on the list.

Therefore, the symbolic meaning of this number is "The fullness of God's people occupying the fullness of God's world".

We also need to look at the names of these tribes. The list is really a combination of two different lists from the Old Testament. There is the original list of "sons of Jacob" (Genesis ch49), which includes Joseph and Levi. Then there is the traditional list of twelve tribes (e.g. Numbers ch1 vv5-15), which omits Levi (set aside as a community of priests) in order to make room for the division of "the house of Joseph". The list in this chapter slightly differs from both.

Ever since the Middle Ages, people have been struck by the omission of Dan. However, we should be focussing on the names rather than the tribes. Close examination of the list shows that the names of Ephraim and Dan have dropped out, and the names of Joseph and Levi have been reinstated. Ephraim and Dan were the locations of the two golden calves established by Jeroboam after the break with Jerusalem. Joseph is famous for rejecting the advances of an adulterous woman. In the person of Phinehas, Levi was outstandingly loyal in the affair at Shittim; "Behold, I give to him my covenant of peace... because he was jealous for his God"

(Numbers ch25 vv12-13). In short, two names associated with unfaithfulness have been replaced by two names associated with faithfulness. This can hardly be a coincidence. The implication is that this list identifies a version of "God's people" which has been cleansed of unfaithfulness.

We already know that they've been "sealed" by God, through the Spirit, as belonging to Christ. In the words of one of Cranmer's prayers, they are "the blessed company of all faithful people".

The scene is also an echo of one of Ezekiel's visions. There the Lord is on the verge of sending his wrath against Jerusalem on account of its various idolatries. He gives instructions, before this happens, to put a mark on the foreheads of all those who "sigh and groan over all the abominations." That is, their loyalty to God makes them grieve over the unfaithfulness of the rest of the city. The purpose of the mark is to protect them from the action of wrath (Ezekiel ch9 vv4-6). Evidently the act of sealing has the same purpose. These people are under spiritual protection. We are told, in ch9, that the sting of the locusts cannot harm them, but I intend to explain the locusts as a spiritual ordeal.

Another obvious parallel is the mark placed on the hands or foreheads of the followers of the Beast, in ch13. In the background of both, we should recognise the repeated command of Deuteronomy about the words of God; "You shall bind them as a sign upon your hand, and they shall be as frontlets before your eyes" (Deuteronomy ch6 v8). They are alternative bonds of loyalty, another of the "opposing pairs" of Revelation. Those who receive the seal will not receive the mark, and that is their spiritual protection. The function of the work of sealing is to bring into existence a body of believers who will remain faithful in the overwhelming time of trial.

V9 "After this I looked, and behold a great multitude… standing before the throne and before the Lamb. Clad in white robes."

This development is also explained in Ephesians. We were sealed with the promised Holy Spirit, as already mentioned. In addition, the God who made us alive together with Christ "raised us up with him, and made us sit with him in the heavenly places in Christ Jesus" (Ephesians ch2v6).

Similarly, Jesus says of those little ones who believe in him that their "angels" (i.e. their representatives) "always behold the face of my Father who is in heaven" (Matthew ch18 v10). So this crowd can be identified as the "presence in heaven" of those who have just been sealed. They are the same people, dwelling on earth and in heaven at the same time. I can disregard the pedantic objection about the clash between "144,000" and "which no man could number", because I've already accounted for 144,000 as a purely symbolic number.

*"From all tribes and peoples and tongues."*
This is the same extent as the authority of the Beast in ch13, the same catchment area, which highlights the competition between the two spheres of loyalty.

For that reason, perhaps, we will see this group on four different occasions. We see them here, immediately following the sealing of the servants of God. We see them in ch14, immediately following the account of the Beast and its "war on the saints", and immediately preceding the proclamation of the fall of Babylon. On that appearance, they are specifically identified as the 144,000. We will see them in ch15, at the beginning of the destruction of Babylon, and finally in ch19 immediately following the fall of Babylon. They are following the progress of the conflict, step by step.

*"Clothed in white robes, with palm branches in their hands, and crying out with a loud voice "Salvation belongs to our God who sits upon the throne, and to the Lamb!"*
This is an echo of Jesus entering Jerusalem for the celebration of his last Passover. Their cry is an expanded version of "Hosanna", now updated from urgent plea to triumphant declaration. The implication is that they are in the heavenly Jerusalem. Their robes are white, as we learn in v14, because they've been "washed in the blood of the Lamb". In other words, they are redeemed, purged of their sin by the death and resurrection of Christ.

Vv13-14 "One of the elders addressed me, saying 'Who are these… and whence have they come?' I said to him 'Sir, you know.'"

This is an echo of Ezekiel's dialogue in the valley of bones; "Son of man, can these bones live?" "O Lord God, thou knowest. (Ezekiel ch37 v3). The answer, in Ezekiel's vision, is that the bones, the lifeless body of God's people, are revived by the power in the Spirit of God. The parallel implies that the crowd in John's vision have passed from the sphere of death to the sphere of life by the power of the same Spirit.

*"These are they who have come out of [EK] the great tribulation."*

The elder then answers both his own questions. I take this to mean that they've had experience of the tribulation. They've passed through it, as it were, and come out the other side. It cannot mean that they've managed to avoid it altogether. The EK will not mean that (and it isn't the way that God works, but that issue ought to be treated as a separate topic).

V15 "Therefore are they before the throne of God, and serve him day and night within his temple."

As promised in one of the letters; "I will make him a pillar in the temple of my God, never shall he go out of it" (ch3 v12).

V16 "They shall hunger no more, neither thirst any more; the sun shall not strike them, nor any scorching heat."

This quotes Isaiah's promise at the time of the original redemption from Babylon; "They shall neither hunger nor thirst, neither scorching wind nor sun shall smite them" (Isaiah ch49 v10).

V17 "For the Lamb in the midst of the throne will be their shepherd, and he will guide them to springs of living water."

This is an echo of Psalm 23, of course, modified by the rest of the Isaiah verse; "For he who has pity on them will lead them and by springs of water will guide them." The addition of the word "living" (as against the still waters of the Psalm) is prompted by the promise of Jesus to the woman of Samaria- "a spring of water welling up to eternal life" (John ch4 v10, v14).

*"And God will wipe away every tear from their eye."*

This alludes, finally, to what may be the greatest and most important promise found in the Old Testament; "And he will destroy on this mountain the covering that is cast over all the peoples, the veil that is spread over all nations. He will swallow up death for ever, and the Lord God will wipe away tears from all faces, and the reproach of his people he will take away from all the earth" (Isaiah ch25 vv7-8).

In short, this crowd, "the blessed company of all faithful people", will experience the life promised to the redeemed.

# 7

# THE CATASTROPHE

## (Revelation Chapter 8)

V1 "When the Lamb opened the seventh seal…"

Here is one of the pivot points of the book of Revelation. The opening of the seventh seal will bring in the seven trumpets, and the sounding of the seventh trumpet will bring in the pouring of the seven bowls. This act is releasing the contents of
the rest of the book.

*"There was silence in heaven for about half an hour."*

This interval takes place before the appearance of the trumpets. The enigmatic statement can be explained by reference to the rest of Revelation.

Firstly, we must notice that in v5, when the trumpets are about to blow, there will be peals of thunder, voices, flashes of lightning, and an earthquake. The same kind of thing happens after the last of the trumpets, and again after the last of the bowls, signalling the approach of judgement. In other words, there is corresponding noise in heaven when God's wrath is acting upon the earth. The obvious conclusion is that "silence in heaven" obliquely indicates a time when God's wrath is *not* acting upon the earth.

Then we are told later that the ten kings "receive authority as kings for one hour, together with the Beast" (ch17 v12). If we see "one hour" in part of Revelation, and "half an hour" in another, it seems reasonable to suppose that the two are connected. That is, the overall statement carries the meaning "The Beast rules for a certain period of time, and for the first half of that period God does not trouble it, does not try to destroy its power." The time of truce continues, so that there is a period of relative tranquillity between the two bouts of havoc and destruction.

As a comparison, let's look at the future ruler featured in Daniel. For a period which is called "one week", he has a "strong covenant with many" on which his power must be based. For half of that week, that is the second half, he is at war with God. Like his model, Antiochus Epiphanes, "he shall cause sacrifice and offerings to cease". The implication is that his rule in the first half of the week, before he starts messing with religious things, will be undisturbed (Daniel ch9 v27).

It looks as if the reign of the Beast follows the same pattern. His Hour is the Daniel king's Week, and is roughly divided in the same way. The remainder of this book is about the second half of the Hour, the Beast at war with God and God's response. This verse alone covers the first "half an hour" before he makes his challenge.

V2 "Then I saw the seven angels who stand before God, and seven trumpets were given to them."

The seven trumpets will be proclaiming catastrophe. At first glance, the next few chapters look like a random series of catastrophes. However, I think they need to be understood as one devastating catastrophe of the natural world, described in several different ways. This is what happens when God brings his power to bear on the destruction of the kingdom of the Beast. In that function, they are very closely associated with the seven "bowls".

These two sequences, the trumpets and the bowls, are so similar that they are often regarded as duplicate versions of the same story. But the real clue to the relationship is that the state of the world after the bowls is considerably worse than the state of the world after the trumpets. The most obvious example is the way the condition of the sea deteriorates. I see them, then, as the beginning and end points of the same set of events, with each trumpet/bowl combination representing a different aspect of the process. On that basis, I feel entitled to cross-reference between the two sequences, and use them to throw light on each other.

V3 "Another angel… was given much incense to mingle with the prayers of the saints."

The prayers of the saints are appealing for God's help against the Beast's equivalent of the "abomination of desolation". Though never mentioned explicitly, that is the act that breaks the truce and leads the world into the tribulation.

V7 "The first angel blew his trumpet, and there followed hail and fire, mixed with blood, which fell upon the earth; and a third of the earth was burnt up, and a third of the trees were burnt up, and all green grass was burnt up."

It should not be necessary, though nowadays it may be necessary, to point out that the trumpets are not heard by the peoples of the earth. There is no suggestion of that. They are simply marking out stages within the vision, for the benefit of John and his readers.

The hail and fire echo one of the Exodus plagues; "The Lord sent hail, and fire ran down to the earth" (Exodus ch9 v23). Similarly the main feature of the first bowl is an outbreak of "foul and evil sores", which echoes another plague; "It became boils breaking out in evil sores on man and beast" (Exodus ch9 v10). So the first item in the sequence is really about the meaning of the sequence. It is a kind of "signature", offering symbolism which points us towards the Exodus. The implication is that the Revelation events, too, are about the redemption of God's people from oppression.

We also have symbolism pointing us towards the judgement of Babylon. After the second trumpet, "something like a great mountain, burning with fire, was thrown down into the sea" (v8). This echoes the warning of Jeremiah; "Behold, I am against you, O destroying mountain (says the Lord) which destroys the whole earth. I will stretch out my hand against you and roll you down from the crags and make you a burnt mountain" (Jeremiah ch51 v25). The implication is that the Revelation events, too, are about the downfall of an idolatrous and oppressive power.

We also have symbolism pointing us towards the condemnation of adultery. The star Wormwood has the effect of making the waters bitter and poisonous (v11). This echoes Jeremiah's warning to the people of

Judah, who have "stubbornly followed their own hearts and gone after the Baals... Therefore thus says the Lord of hosts, the God of Israel; Behold, I will feed this people with wormwood and give them poisonous water to drink" (Jeremiah ch9 vv14-15). This is an allusion to the ritual of the "water of bitterness", prescribed in Numbers ch5 as a way to test a wife suspected of adultery. The implication is that the Revelation events, too, are a way of chastising the spiritual infidelity of a people from whom the Lord expects loyalty.

The remaining trumpets of this chapter cover, in turn, the sea, the land (seen through the rivers) and the heavens. Here is another instance, then, of Revelation's "heavens, land and sea" division of the created universe. Also a duplication of the "something burning, falling down" image. That's why I take these events to be a single devastating event, seen as it were from three different camera angles.

Regarding this chapter as prophecy, we can only speculate about the nature of an event portrayed in these half-metaphorical terms. Let's consider, first, a damage assessment. As regards the land, one third of the earth, together with its vegetation, has been burnt up. One third of the sea has become blood. In the heavens, the sun, the moon and the stars have lost a third of their brightness. This is really about the atmosphere, since the most "economical" way of achieving this effect would be by pollution blocking the light. The general result is that all three regions have been spoiled.

If these effects have a single cause, it would have to be a large-scale event, something capable of having a massive and ultimately fatal impact upon the planet at large. I'm going to examine four plausible possibilities (because I can't resist the symmetry of the number) which have been suggested from time to time. I'll consider them firstly in terms of their potential ability to produce the effects described in this chapter.

*Super-volcano eruption*

This would, of course, be a "burning mountain", almost literally. No obvious reason (apart from possible location) why it should be "thrown into the sea". Land and vegetation in the vicinity would be "burnt up". Volcanic ash in the atmosphere could be blocking out the light, and the settlement of the ash would be responsible for poisoning the rivers and seas. It is tempting to see the image of a volcano in the "smoke arising from the bottomless pit" in the next chapter.

## Asteroid collision

Perhaps this would, even more literally, present the appearance of "a burning mountain thrown into the sea". Less obvious reason why much of the land should be "burnt up". Debris from the impact would provide material in the atmosphere, with the same effect as before. These first two natural events have both been proposed as explanations of the extinction of the dinosaurs.

## Nuclear war

The impact of the weapons themselves would be burning the land and vegetation. The suggestion has been made that smoke and soot from large-scale fires would fill the atmosphere, with the same effect as before. Another suggested side-effect is that the ozone-layer would be depleted on a global scale. This would account for the effect of the fourth bowl, after which the sun "was allowed to scorch men with fire". The natural disasters don't really explain this feature.

## Industrial pollution

This might not need to be a single large event. In the long-term, the accumulating effects of many such events and neglectful practices could be enough, on their own, to spoil the land, pollute the atmosphere, poison the rivers, degenerate the oceans, and deplete the ozone layer. Hence many of the effects described in this chapter. But the events in which "things fall down to the earth" would have to be regarded as symbolic. And there is less obvious reason for the atmosphere of "crisis" implied in this chapter, because the process would be slow-moving and less obvious.

It isn't easy, on that basis, to identify a "most likely" candidate. Another possible approach is to consider which one of them is most likely to happen first. Which one would win the race? I get the impression that super-volcano eruptions are very rare events, which would push that option low down the probability scale. Astronomers take the chances of an asteroid collision more seriously, to the extent of watching the orbits of passing objects very carefully.

If the natural disasters were the only possibilities, nothing in Revelation would oblige us to expect a catastrophe in the near future. But the possibility of human self-destruction brings a new factor into the equation. Putting it bluntly, if Revelation prophecy is to be fulfilled at all, it must be fulfilled while the human race is still in existence. Which means that the prophecies implied in this chapter would have to be fulfilled through the human capacities for self-destruction, unless there was a natural disaster which could move quickly enough to forestall them.

The degradation of the environment by industrial pollution differs from the other possibilities in that it does not require any new "event" to start it off; it only requires that existing trends should continue. So the gradual strangulation of the planet by the effects of human technology does rather look like the "default" option, the most likely outcome if nothing else intervenes first.

V13 "Woe, woe, woe, to those who dwell on earth, at the blasts of the other trumpets which the three angels are about to blow."

The three Woes will be the climax of the Trumpet sequence. Under the outward appearance of new events, they will display the results of the events which have already happened.

# 8

# THE DEVASTATED WORLD

## (Revelation Chapter 9)

The two Woes of this chapter will display the world's reaction to the great earth-catastrophe of the previous chapter. The first Woe is the psychological reaction, and the second Woe is the social reaction.

V1 "And the fifth angel blew his trumpet."

V3 "Then from the smoke came locusts on the earth."

V12 "The first woe has passed."

In order to understand this invasion, we have to consider the different aspects of the description as a whole.

### They are locusts

The text calls them locusts. I understand that some of the details of the description are features which might be found on any ordinary swarm. Ordinary locusts, apparently, have hair and scales, and make a noise in flight, and their normal life-span is around five months, as in this passage. Any locust-swarm would be a source of terror, because locusts will eat up your crops and bring you close to starvation.

### They are not ordinary locusts

But this description has got additional details, bizarre details, which would not be found in any ordinary locust swarm. They appear "like horses, arrayed for battle". They have human faces, with golden crowns. They have the teeth of lions, and stings like scorpions. The noise of their wings has become thunderous. And it seems that everything else about them has been magnified; at least their features are surely much more visible and noticeable than they would have been in locusts of ordinary size.

So the image starts with a topical model (a locust swarm) which would have been a source of terror in its own right. The emotion is then magnified. Further details are thrown into the image to ramp up the intensity of the terror by several degrees.

### They come from "outside"

They originate from the smoke which comes from the bottomless pit. (v2). The word "bottomless" (ABYSSOS) alludes to the "deep" or the "abyss of waters" which appears in the Creation story, pushed back by God to make room for human life. It is the part of Creation which God has not organised, making it the symbol of the source of evil. The sea, in Revelation, has the same overtones, for the same reason. They are under the command of Abaddon or Apollyon, the destroyer or power of destruction, which is the polar opposite of "order".

### They come from God

We're told that the star "was given the key" which opened the shaft of the pit. This is a reverential way of saying that the key came from God, which means that the locusts have been released on God's authority. The same applies when we read that the locusts "were given power" and "were allowed to torture" (v3, v5).

It is also important to recognise, in the background, the invasions described by Joel. The first band of locusts in that book have "lions' teeth" (Joel ch1 v6). As for the second band, "Their appearance is like the appearance of horses", and and they leap on the tops of the mountain "as with the rumbling of chariots" (Joel ch2 vv4-5). Now the locusts in Joel are designated as the Lord's army; "The earth quakes before them, the heavens tremble... The Lord utters his voice before his army, for his host is exceedingly great" (Joel ch2 vv10-11). The implication is that this army of locusts, whatever its immediate origin, is also ultimately acting as God's army and serving his purpose.

*They bring torture*

Whatever they look like, they don't act like locusts. Their impact is on the human population, not the crops. They torture their victims without killing them. The effect of the torture is that "men will seek death". This is the state of mind which we call "despair", and I don't think we need to look any further to identify the nature of the torture. The function of these locusts is that they are the specialised agents and carriers of Despair.

Yet this is no ordinary despair. One might think that "wanting to die" was the deepest, the worst possible, level of despair. But there's a much deeper level indicated in the words that "men will seek death and will not find it". There's no need for us to puzzle our minds about the exact mechanism of "not being able to die". The real point is that this possibility implies an intensity of Despair beyond anything previously experienced, almost beyond anything that could previously be imagined.

Nevertheless, there's a precedent, contained in one of the complaints of Job; "Why is light given to him that is in misery, and life to the bitter in soul, who long for death and it comes not, and dig for it more than for hid treasures; Who rejoice exceedingly, and are glad when they find the grave?... For the thing that I fear comes upon me, and what I dread befalls me. I am not at ease, nor am I quiet; I have no rest; but trouble comes" (Job ch3 vv20-26).

This is not a coincidence, because there's another reference to Job at the same stage in the "bowl" sequence. When the fifth bowl is poured out, we're told that men "cursed the God of heaven for their pain and sores". Of course this is precisely what Job was advised to do when he was suffering the experience of his own sores.

The message seems to be that the population of the world at large is undergoing a collective "Job" experience. The thing they feared has come upon them. They are not at ease and have no rest, and so they long for death. Job was plunged into despair by the fact that his world was falling apart. I suggest that the human race, in this chapter, is plunged into despair for the same reason. The "falling apart" was graphically described in the previous chapter.

Yet we're told that those who have "the seal of God" are immune. They cannot be touched (v4). The torture of Despair is essentially a spiritual attack, against which there is a spiritual defence. The effect of the Holy Spirit would include the confirmation and strengthening of Faith, which is the polar opposite of Despair. They are still putting their trust in the Creator God, whatever else is happening.

V13 "Then the sixth angel blew his trumpet."

V15 "The four angels were released."

Ch11 v14 "The second woe has passed."

In order to understand this invasion, we have to consider the different aspects of the description as a whole.

*They are cavalry*

The text calls them cavalry, and describes them as riding horses. The picture seems to be based on the Parthians, a people ruling the territories eastward of the Roman Empire. Several of these details would have been true about one of their armies. Any Parthian invasion would have been coming from the Euphrates. They would have been wearing armour and fighting on horseback, a style of warfare learned from the nomads on the steppes. They also had a metaphorical "sting in the tail". Their most famous tactical skill was their ability to despatch arrows backwards while riding away from an enemy. At the battle of Carrhae, (53 B.C.), they overwhelmed a force of seven Roman legions and killed the Roman leader Crassus, one of the allies of Julius Caesar. They then attempted to invade Syria, but were beaten off. So the thought of another Parthian invasion would have been a source of terror.

*They are not ordinary cavalry*

But the description has got additional details, bizarre details, which would not be found in an ordinary Parthian army. The horses have lions' heads, with fire and smoke and sulphur coming out of their mouths. Their tails are in the form of serpents, with biting heads of their own. While the size of the army has been magnified, to a much greater size than human armies could muster.

So the image starts with a topical model (a Parthian army) which would have been a source of terror in its own right. The emotion is then magnified. Further details are thrown into the image to ramp up the intensity of the terror by several degrees.

### They come from "outside"

They come from the Euphrates, and presumably from the other side of the Euphrates. At the time when John was writing, the upper Euphrates was the boundary between the Roman province of Syria and the Parthian territory around Edessa. Thus, from the viewpoint of Roman citizens, that far side was a region "outside" the civilised world, the Graeco-Roman world. It would belong to the world of the barbarians, not the world of ordered society. So I recommend that students of Revelation not get fixated on the physical geography of "crossing the Euphrates". The symbolism of the act is more important.

### They come from God

The army is released by a command which comes direct from God's altar, and therefore on God's authority. They are to be released at a specific pre-planned moment- "the hour, the day, the month, and the year" (v15)- which must have been planned by God. (Here, incidentally, is a scriptural endorsement of the day/month/year dating convention.) Also the sheer size of the army confirms that it comes from God. That number of "twice ten thousand times ten thousand" (v16) is an echo of the host which accompanied the Lord when he "came from Sinai into the holy place", namely "twice ten thousand, thousands upon thousands" (Psalm 68 v17). Similarly, when the Ancient of Days took his seat in Daniel's vision, "a thousand thousands served him, and ten thousand times ten thousand stood before him" (Daniel ch7 v10). Only "the Lord of hosts" can muster armies of that order of magnitude. The implication is that these cavalry, too, are acting as God's army and serving his purpose.

### They bring destruction

We're told that this army will be killing one third of mankind. This needs to be understood in the context of the previous trumpets. I interpreted the first four as a description of a major world-catastrophe, whether natural or man-made. There seemed to be an impact on the planet at large, setting in motion the spoiling of the land, the sea, and the atmosphere. the kind of process which could ultimately render the earth almost uninhabitable. I understand the fifth trumpet as a portrait of a state of intense despair, the first human reaction to this event.

I now suggest that the sixth trumpet is describing the social impact of the fifth trumpet. It's about the effect of despair on the bonds of human society. We must return to the point that this army is crossing the perceived border between the world of social order and the barbarian world "outside". So we might see in this cavalry a representation of all those forces which come from "outside" the social order, and which would have the effect of undermining it. These have never been completely absent from human life, but they would be released in full force in the kind of emergency which these chapters appear to be describing. The predominance of despair would undermine the motivation to keep things going.

In short, I understand this army as the collective symbol of all those forces which would have the effect of bringing human society crashing down into anarchy, and which would *thus* bring about the death of "one third of mankind".

The account of the Witnesses (ch11) has been inserted between this description and the announcement that the Second Woe is complete. This implies that renewed persecution of the church is one of the symptoms of the social breakdown. A panic-stricken world is finding reasons to direct blame and hostility against the Christian community, just as they were doing in the middle of the troubles of the Roman world.

### They bring a call to repentance

The army of locusts was an echo of the army of locusts in Joel, and the appearance of a pair of invading armies, coming in succession, is also an echo of the pattern in Joel. Now the function of the armies in Joel was that they were a call to repentance; "Yet even now (says the Lord) return to me with all your heart, with fasting and with weeping and with mourning" (Joel ch2 v12). "But now he commands all men everywhere to repent"

(Acts ch17 v30). The implication is that the combined armies here have the same function. However, the opportunity to repent is not taken in this chapter;

Vv20-21 "The rest of mankind...did not repent of the works of their hands nor give up worshipping demons...nor did they repent of their murders or their sorceries or their immorality or their thefts."

*Stephen Disraeli*

# 9

# TIME RUNNING OUT

## (Revelation Chapter 10)

The message of this chapter comes through John's encounter with a great angel, which echoes and "updates" a couple of similar encounters in the Old Testament.

V1 I saw another mighty angel coming down from heaven, wrapped up in a cloud with a rainbow over his head and his face was like the sun."

The description of the angel echoes details from a number of passages, from the Old Testament and from earlier chapters in this book. When Ezekiel met the likeness of the glory of the Lord, in his first vision, the appearance of his brightness was "like the appearance of the bow that is in the cloud on the day of rain" (Ezekiel ch1 v28).

We've already seen the rainbow round the throne in the fourth chapter of this book, while the face of the angel of Jesus in the first chapter was "like the sun shining in full strength". In a moment, he will be calling out "with a loud voice, like a lion roaring", an apparent reference to "the lion of the tribe of Judah" in the fifth chapter. Evidently this angel does not represent a lowly subordinate.

V2 "He had a little scroll open in his hand."

This detail sets up the re-enactment of a scene from Ezekiel's vision.

"His legs like pillars of fire… He set his right foot on the sea and his left foot on the land."

This recalls the vision of the last three chapters of Daniel. The prophet encounters a man, clothed in linen, whose arms and legs have a brightness "like the gleam of burnished bronze" (Daniel ch10 vv4-6). The figure is standing above the waters of the stream (Daniel ch12 v6), showing his authority over the Tigris, and indeed over the whole power of Babylon. The angel in this chapter, planting his feet on sea and land, is firmly demonstrating sovereignty over both regions. Including, presumably, the Beast from the sea and the Beast from the land, who appear in a later chapter.

Vv3-4 "He called out with a loud voice... when he called out, the seven thunders sounded... I was about to write, but I heard a voice from heaven saying 'Seal up what the seven thunders have said and do not write it down."

The voice of seven thunders would have to be God's voice, of course, the expression of God's will. The command sounds a little strange. Not because of the secrecy (we expect God to have secrets) but because it prompts the question; "Why is John hearing these words, in the first place, if he's not allowed to report them?" There must be something we're intended to learn from the very fact that these thunders have spoken, regardless of the content. The most plausible explanation is that they are expressing God's will for judgement, which will take effect at the sounding of the seventh trumpet. This is then reflected in the angel's announcement, and we have no "need to know" about the details.

V6 "The angel swore by him who lives for ever and ever, who created heaven and what is in it, the earth and what is in it, and the sea and what is in it."

A timely reminder that the Creator of the world, all three regions of the world, is controlling this judgement of the world.

*"... that there should be no more delay."*
This is the "updating" of an announcement at the end of Daniel's vision. Daniel had asked "the man clothed in linen" the very important question; "How long shall it be before the end of these wonders?" Then that figure swore "by him who lives for ever that it will be for a time, two times, and half a time" In other words, three and a half times. This is traditionally, and I believe rightly, identified with the "half a week" or

three and a half days during which the hostile ruler is at war with his God.. Once the end of that period was reached, "the shattering of the power of the holy people" would come to an end, and "all these things would be accomplished" (Daniel ch12 vv6-7).

The phrase translated "no more delay" is literally "time no longer" [KAIROS OUKETI]. That is, the sequence of "times" anticipated in Daniel has now drawn to a close. So when the seventh angel sounds the seventh trumpet, "the mystery of God should be fulfilled". The world would then see the fulfilment of what was promised at the climax of Daniel. Following the intervention of God, the power of the hostile ruler would be overthrown and the "holy people" would be restored.

V8 "Go take the scroll which is open in the hand of the angel."

This echoes, and begins to "update", the command given to Ezekiel in his first vision. He was told to take the scroll and eat it, and then to go and speak "my words" to the house of Israel. So the scroll represents the word of God, which supplied the content of his message. The task was easier than it might have been, because Ezekiel was not being sent "to a people of foreign speech and a hard language", but to his own countrymen, who should be able to understand him. Nevertheless, he will find them unwilling to listen, because "the house of Israel are of a hard forehead and of a stubborn heart". The taste of the scroll had been sweet, because it was the Word of God. But Ezekiel left the meeting "in bitterness of my heart in the heat of my spirit", which is very understandable, given the terms of his task. He was advised later that he will be addressing two kinds of people, viz. the "wicked" and those among the "righteous" who have fallen into sin (Ezekiel ch3, passim).

V11 "You must again prophesy about many peoples and nations and tongues and kings".

"Again" is highlighting the fact that John's task is a fresh version of Ezekiel's task. "Many tongues" is the difference, because John will be addressing the world at large instead of a single people. Otherwise, we may assume, the mission will be the same. "Words of warning and lamentation and woe". The prophet being sent both to the wicked and to the righteous who have fallen into sin, the task in both cases being to call them to repentance. Almost certainly finding most of them "of a hard forehead and of a stubborn heart" and unwilling to listen.

This mission , the final call to repentance, is made appropriate by the imminent judgement implied in the prospect of the "seventh trumpet". If the kingdom of the Beast is going to be cleared away, then this will be their final opportunity. Looking ahead, this would be the work of the "two witnesses" in the next chapter.

Finally, I'd like to suggest a supplementary interpretation of the seven thunders, based on the "covenant" theme. That "rainbow" symbol first appears in Genesis, as the token of God's covenant with Noah and with the rest of mankind. We're told that when God showed his power at Sinai "Moses spoke, and God answered him in thunder" (Exodus ch19 v19), and this exchange was the precursor of God's covenant with Israel. Perhaps, then, these thunders are also pointing towards a new covenant relationship, following on from the time of judgment.

The Christian church knows of one new covenant made possible through Christ. But the description at the end of Revelation suggests that conditions in the "new Jerusalem", in the presence of God, could be a closer fulfilment of the kind of "new covenant" promised by Jeremiah, when men would not sin - "I will put my law within them"- , and evangelism would no longer be necessary "for they shall all know me"- (Jeremiah ch31 vv33-34).

John finds the scroll sweet in his mouth, as Ezekiel did, but bitter in his stomach. No doubt the difficulty of the task, as well as the harshness of the message, would account for the bitterness, as in Ezekiel's case. Yet the implicit promise of the restoration of God's people is part of the sweetness.

# 10

# THE TWO WITNESSES

## (Revelation Chapter 11)

I must admit, from the outset (to avoid any possible disappointment) that I won't be treating the Two Witnesses as two distinct individuals. I regard them as God's faithful, witnessing church experiencing the climax of the tribulation. They are represented by a double symbol because they have a double function, or even two double functions. Therefore anyone who announces himself as one of the Two Witnesses, except in that corporate sense, is claiming for himself more than God has given him.

V1 "I was given a measuring rod like a staff and I was told 'Rise and measure the temple of God and the altar and those what worship there"
This is an echo of the measuring of the temple which Ezekiel witnessed in vision (Ezekiel ch40).Ezekiel's temple was being measured out because the Lord was going to return to it (Ezekiel ch43 vv1-5), so this measuring also prefigures the Lord's return.
But what is meant by "temple", in the context of the New Testament? Paul tells the Corinthians that they, the community of Christ, are in themselves the temple of God, as a corporate body. He's been developing the metaphor of "building" the church, and then he draws attention to the fact that this building has a divine resident; "Do you not know that you [plural] are God's temple, and that God's Spirit dwells in you [plural]?" That is why division within the community is such a grievous offence to God. It is tantamount to the sacrilegious destruction of a temple (1 Corinthians ch3 vv16-17).
Paul uses the word "temple" again in connection with the "man of lawlessness" (2 Thessalonians ch2 v4), but I suggest that this reference

and the reference in the present chapter both need to be understood in terms of the explanation in 1 Corinthians. The "temple" in each passage is the worshipping community itself. In which case neither reference demands (or predicts) the building of any physical temple to replace the one destroyed in A.D. 70.

V2 "But do not measure the court outside the temple. Leave that out, for it is given over to the nations."

If this chapter and the passage in 2 Thessalonians were both talking about a literal, physical temple, they would be contradicting one another. Paul says that the "man of lawlessness" takes his seat in the temple. John says that the hostile power does not get that far. We escape the conflict by assuming that both passages are using metaphor, handled in two slightly different ways.

My solution is that "the temple" in 2 Thessalonians and the "outer courts" in this chapter are the same place, viz. the outward fabric of the church, including the organisational structure. Human-based authority could control that much by compulsion, or even win cooperation from the leadership and some of the members. However, human authority cannot command the hearts of believers, and there would be a less visible, faithful remnant. Hence the implied promise that the nations are excluded from the spiritual core of the temple, "the altar and those who worship there."

*"They will trample over the holy city."*

This repeats the warning that Jerusalem will be "trodden down by the Gentiles" (Luke ch21 v24). Both passages are echoing the prophet's complaint about the Babylonians; "Thy holy people possesses the sanctuary a little while; our adversaries have trodden it down" (Isaiah ch63 v18). If the image here was inspired by the events of A.D. 70, then the message for the faithful of John's time would be that the spiritual life of Israel has been preserved in the church.

But there's also an echo of another kind of unwelcome presence; "Who requires of you this trampling on my courts?" (Isaiah ch1 v12). That's part of God's complaint about his own people, that their lives of immorality and injustice and unfaithfulness have been invalidating their worship. The implication is that God's holy place in this chapter is being overrun in both ways.

*"Forty-two months".*

The tribulation period in Revelation is given three different time-labels. All three of them go back to Daniel's "half a week" during which the sacrifice, or the worship of God, is interrupted. That is three and a half days, or three and a half years out of a "week of years". Hence "a time, two times, and half a time" (three and a half times) which is given as an alternative in Daniel ch12, and also used in Revelation ch12. Three and a half years is forty-two months, as here. Assuming a thirty-day month, forty-two months are one thousand, two hundred and sixty days, as in the next verse. So all these time-labels, whenever they appear in Revelation, relate to the same period, and carry the simple meaning "this passage is about the tribulation of the church." There is no value in transposing them as literal time-periods into past history or future history and trying to calculate dates for the events of "the end-times". We don't need those dates, and scripture is not offering to supply them.

V3 "And I will give my two witnesses power to prophesy for one thousand two hundred and sixty days, clothed in sackcloth"

During this time of tribulation, God's faithful church worshipping round "the altar", spiritually protected but not physically protected, come out into the world to witness to the world. The meaning of the sackcloth is that their message is the general need of repentance, in which they include themselves.

V4 "These are the two olive trees and the two lampstands which stand before the Lord of the earth".

This is a direct reference to the vision of Zechariah ch4 in which the prophet is told to identify the olive trees and lampstand with "the two anointed who stand by the Lord of the whole earth". For Zechariah's message, the two "anointed ones" are the king and the high priest. That is to say, they are Zerubbabel, the Davidic prince, and Joshua (though the Persians won't allow Zerubbabel to be called king).

What does "king and high priest" mean in the New Testament? The first obvious answer is that both terms refer to Christ. But the combination recurs in the earlier scene around God's throne, with reference to the elders who represent God's people. As I observed, we know them as kings, because they wear crowns. And we know them as priests, I believe, because there are twenty-four of them, which is the number of the Old Testament priestly families. They themselves then proclaim, on behalf of God's people, that Christ has redeemed men and made them "a kingdom and priests for our God". Or "kings and priests", in some texts and translations. (ch5 v10). That is the chain of evidence leading to my conclusion that "the two anointed ones" are a symbol of the faithful community as a body.

V5 "If anyone would harm them fire pours from their mouths and consumes their foes."

This is a power which was given, metaphorically, to Jeremiah. For when the people disregarded his warnings and asserted that the Lord would do nothing, the Lord's response was to say to the prophet; "Because they have spoken this word, behold, I am making my words in your mouth a fire, and this people wood, and the fire shall devour them" (Jeremiah ch5 v14). The point being that Jeremiah's warnings of judgement would be vindicated. When that power is visualised in the case of the two witnesses, it implies a similar promise.

V6 "They have power to shut the sky that no rain may fall… they have power over the waters to turn them into blood and to smite the earth with every plague."

These are the powers which were given to Elijah and Moses respectively. Is that a reason to identify them literally as Elijah and Moses returning to the earth? No, because they appear to be sharing both sets of powers jointly (besides sharing the powers of Jeremiah), instead of holding their own separately.

The powers should be seen as an indirect way of announcing that the Two Witnesses are resuming the tasks of Moses and Elijah. The chief task of Moses was to stand up against the oppression of God's people coming from hostile power. The chief task of Elijah was to stand up against the temptation of God's people coming from alien religion. Between them, they cover the external danger and the internal danger to the integrity of the community. The seven churches addressed at the beginning of the book were being warned about the proximity of both kinds of danger. Similarly the tribulation would be presenting both kinds of danger, and the situation would require both kinds of witness.

In summary, the Witnesses have a two-fold status as "kings and priests" in Christ, and they are giving the two-fold testimony of Moses and Elijah, and that is why we see two of them.

V7 "The Beast that ascends from the bottomless pit will make war on them and conquer them and kill them."

It's very telling that the Greek word for "witness" has become the English word "martyr". In the middle of a tribulation, one leads on to the other. We will meet "the Beast from the sea" in ch13. For prophetic symbolism, as I've remarked already, "the sea" and "the bottomless pit" are the same place, the notional source of evil.

V8 "Their dead bodies will lie in the street of the great city which is allegorically called Sodom and Egypt, where their Lord was crucified.".

The identity of the city is ambiguous. Naming it after Sodom and Egypt suggests a place of sin and persecution. The place "where their Lord was crucified", taken literally, would mean Jerusalem. But in the rest of Revelation, the phrase "great city" belongs to Babylon, and therefore to Rome.

One possible solution is to suppose that John's understanding of the "great city" is like John Bunyan's understanding of that "Vanity Fair", where Christian and Faithful were put on trial. That is to say, it does not indicate any particular city, but rather indicates "the world", seen as a city. Thus it would be "the world" that crucified the Lord, and "the world" that persecutes his followers. That's in keeping with my premise that the Two Witnesses are the faithful community as a body, in which case they would not be getting killed in one location. The earth in general would be the place of their martyrdom.

V9 "For three and a half days, men...gaze at their dead bodies and refuse to let them be placed in a tomb."

One effect of refusing burial is that the world is exposing the bodies to the air, and allowing the blood of the murdered faithful to "cry to the Lord for vengeance". The body of a lawfully executed man must be buried on the same day, to conceal it from the sight of God and perhaps, partly, to debar such an appeal (Deuteronomy ch21 v23). Thus the world is unconsciously acknowledging that these people were killed unlawfully. Three and a half days amount to half a week, so this is yet another of the time-labels identifying the period of the tribulation.

V10 "Those who dwell on the earth will rejoice over them and make merry and exchange presents."

This is an echo in reverse of what happened when Ezra proclaimed the law; "And all the people went their way to eat and drink and to send portions and to make great rejoicing" (Nehemiah ch8 v12). In this verse, the inhabitants of the earth are celebrating their lawlessness. But their rejoicing will be found to be premature.

*"These two prophets had been a torment to those who dwell on the earth."*

They are tormented in their consciences by appeals to repent, because they do not want to repent (see ch9 vv20-21). That is what motivates them to angry hostility. They are also scared and angered by their helplessness in the great world-catastrophe of the Seven Trumpets, so they may well be prone to make the faithful their scapegoats. This is what was happening in the time of Tertullian; "If the Tiber rises, if the Nile does not rise, if the heavens give no rain, if there is an earthquake, famine, or pestilence, straightway the cry is 'Christians to the lion!'" (Apology, ch40).

Vv11-12 "A breath of life from God entered into them, and they stood up on their feet... And in the face of their foes they went up to heaven in a cloud."

The first stage of that process echoes the restoration of God's people in Ezekiel's "valley of bones" vision; "The breath came into them and they lived, and stood upon their feet" (Ezekiel ch37 v10). The second stage shows, by anticipation, the fulfilment of Paul's promise relating to the Return of Christ; "And the dead in Christ shall rise first; then we who are alive shall be caught up together with them in the clouds to meet the Lord in the air" (1 Thessalonians ch4 vv16-17). This is the only "rapture" known to the New Testament.

V13 "There was a great earthquake."
God's response in judgement.

V14 "The second woe has passed."
As already observed, the second woe proper is the social breakdown of the world in the face of the world-catastrophe. The tribulation suffered by the church is part of the experience of the social breakdown.

V15 "Then the seventh angel blew his trumpet, and there were loud voices in heaven saying 'The kingdom of the world has become the kingdom of our Lord and of his Christ."
In other words, the request in the Lord's prayer, "Thy kingdom come", has now been answered. This is it. The blowing of the seventh trumpet is the grand climax of the campaign.

V17 "We give thanks to thee, Lod God Almighty, who art and who wast, that thou hast taken thy great power and begun to reign.".
The twenty-four elders continue the praise. The original formula of ch1 was "who is and who was and who is to come." In this verse, the "future" part of the formula has been left out. His reigning in full power is no longer a future expectation but a present reality. The remainder of their song echoes the words of the psalm which tells how the nations raged and the kings of the earth set themselves "against the Lord and his anointed" (Psalm 2 v2), and which then goes on to record the Lord's promise of power to his anointed son.

Then the elders proclaim (and the noisy activities of the last verse of the chapter carry the same message) that the time of judgement has come. The servants of the Lord will be rewarded, and the destroyers of the earth will be destroyed.

Wait one moment, though. If this is the grand climax, the arrival of the End, why are we still only halfway through the book, with eleven chapters to go? The answer is that we have arrived at the beginning of the End. There is a tail-piece in the form of the Seven Bowls. If the Trumpets indicate the last hour of unredeemed human history, the Bowls are the fifty-ninth minute of that hour. The last four chapters cover the return of Christ and what follows. Everything else is commentary or explanation relating to the delivery of God's judgement.

For example, the main sequence of the narrative is interrupted at the end of this chapter (to be resumed in ch14). The next two chapters are what film-makers would call a "flashback" sequence. They have the usual function of flashbacks, in that they are explaining the background of the events which have already been seen. In this case, the church needs to understand how the tribulation has been Satan's vindictive response to the Atonement.

# 11

# THE WOMAN AND THE DRAGON

## (Revelation Chapter 12)

V1 "And a great portent appeared in heaven, a woman clothed with the sun, with the moon under her feet, and on her head a crown of twelve stars."

Joseph had a dream in which the sun and moon and eleven stars were bowing down to him, and this was interpreted as referring to Jacob and Rachel, his parents, and his eleven brothers (Genesis ch37 vv9-10).

In this vision, Joseph implicitly re-joins the other stars, and they are crowning a woman who must represent God's people. We may take the moon as representing Rachel, the mother of Israel. Strictly speaking, she was not the only mother of the sons of Jacob, but the Joseph story ignores that point. The woman in this vision is clothed with the sun, which tends to be the property of Christ in this book (see, for example, ch1 v17). The moon is under her feet, which may mean that God's people with Christ are taking precedence over God's people without Christ.

V2 "She cried out in her pangs of birth, in anguish for delivery."

We must see in the background two passages from the prophets. The first is Jeremiah's judgement on Jerusalem, threatened by the Babylonians; "And you, O desolate one, what do you mean that you dress in scarlet, that you deck yourself with ornaments of gold, that you enlarge your eyes with paint? In vain you beautify yourself. Your lovers despise you, they seek your life.

For I heard a cry as of a woman in travail, anguish as of one bringing forth her first child, the cry of the daughter of Zion gasping for breath, stretching out her hands, 'Woe is me, I am fainting before murderers'" (Jeremiah ch4 vv30-31).

The above has vital importance for the book of Revelation. In effect, the woman in this vision and the woman in the vision of ch17 have divided up the passage between them. This woman has taken the second verse, the verse of "giving birth" and "suffering at the hands of the enemy". While "the other woman" (in the full colloquial sense) is clearly modelled on the first verse, the Harlot verse. This makes them another of the contrasting pairs of Revelation, representing respectively the faithful and unfaithful Jerusalem, the faithful and unfaithful versions of God's people. There are overtones also of the contrast between Wisdom and the adulterous Folly in Proverbs.

The other reference point is Micah's prophecy. The daughter of Zion is told to "writhe and groan like a woman in travail", as she leaves the city and departs for Babylon, where the Lord will redeem her from her enemies (Micah ch4 v10). In the next chapter, the woman in travail "gives birth", apparently to the event of the return from exile. However, this passage also includes the well-known prophecy that one who is to be ruler in Israel will come forth from Bethlehem (Micah ch5 vv2-3). From the Christian viewpoint, then, a combination of the two themes "giving birth to salvation" and "giving birth to Jesus".

In the rest of this chapter, there will be a close association between the birth-pangs of "suffering" and the birth-pangs of "salvation".

V3 "And another portent appeared in heaven; behold, a great red dragon, with seven heads and ten horns and seven diadems upon his heads."

The dragon is Leviathan, whom the Lord will slay when his "day" comes (Isaiah ch27 v1). Amongst other things, Leviathan is the mythical monster that wants to swallow up the sun, in eclipse, and prevent the arrival of the light (Job ch3 v8).

The colour of the dragon is the colour of the horse "permitted to take peace from the earth" in ch6.The crowned heads represent royal authority, and horns are the standard Biblical image of power. "Ten horns" means that the power is worldwide, but "seven heads" means that the authority remains nevertheless under God's control. Focussing on the symbolism of number, we don't need to worry about distributing the ten horns among the seven heads. The rest of the chapter is about the struggle between these two portents.

V4 "His tail swept down a third of the stars of heaven."
The traditional interpretation, as found in Milton, is that Satan's rebellion brought in one third of God's host of angels. However, the rebellion of Satan before the foundation of the world is a fantasy without genuine Biblical support. It's better, I think, to find the stars in Daniel's promise; "And those who are wise shall shine like the brightness of the firmament, and those who turn many to righteousness, like the stars for ever and ever" (Daniel ch12 v3). In other words, this is the approximate proportion of infidelity that will be found among God's people.

*"And the dragon stood before the woman... that he might devour her child."*
Ready to swallow up the sun.

V5 "She brought forth a male child, one who is to rule the nations with a rod of iron, but her child was caught up to God and to his throne."
"You are my son, today I have begotten you... you shall break [the nations] with a rod of iron" (Psalm 2 vv7-9). Being born, being the Son, ascending into heaven. This is the recognisable outline of the story of Jesus. In the next few verses, we shall see the effects of his death.
Does this mean that all these details really do belong to the iconography about the Blessed Virgin, as in the Catholic tradition? If the child is Jesus, must the mother be Mary? No, because that conflicts with her symbolic status as the direct counterpart of the Harlot. She is "the Jerusalem above" (Galatians ch4 v26). She is becoming the church of Christ, sitting "in the heavenly places in Christ Jesus" (Ephesians ch2 v6). In the next verse she flees into the wilderness, and her experience there is the kind of thing that happens to a symbolic figure, not a real human individual.

Her exile in the wilderness, nourished by God, is labelled as one thousand two hundred and sixty days (v6) or as "a time, times, and half a time" (v14). In other words, this is the period of the tribulation.

V7 "Now war rose in heaven, Michael and his angels fighting against the dragon."

Michael represents the power of God to stand up and fight for his people (Daniel ch12 v1).

V9 "And the great dragon was thrown down… who is called the Devil and Satan, the deceiver of the whole world."

V10 "The accuser of our brethren has been thrown down, who accuses them day and night before our God."

The defeat of Satan is also hailed in the story of the seventy disciples (the number of God's mission to the whole world). When they return to Jesus, he assures them "I saw Satan fall like lightning from heaven" (Luke ch10 v18). Jesus would not have been choosing that moment to reminisce about events before the Creation. His meaning must be that Satan began falling during their mission, and as a result of their mission.

We need to understand that the fall of Satan is a fall from power. We must look into the source of Satan's power, to discover how that power may be defeated. He is named in Hebrew as the "adversary", in the sense of being the opposing party in a court of law. His function in the first chapter of Job is to make our sins known to God and draw them to his attention.

There's an illustration of this in Zechariah ch3, where Joshua the high priest stands in the presence of God, and Satan stands at his right hand to accuse him. The intended charge is not a false accusation, because Joshua's iniquity is clearly visible, symbolised by his filthy garments. Here is a picture of the Accuser's hold over humanity, not much different from that of an informant or a blackmailer. It is based on possession of damaging information about human sin. Or, to be exact, it is based on the existence of human sin, about which damaging information can be possessed.

The same story shows that the best way of dealing with a blackmailer is to make his information useless. The garments which represent Joshua's iniquity are removed and replaced by clean ones. Satan's evidence has been taken away from him, and he stands rebuked and silenced. In the same way, the mission of the seventy was presenting, on behalf of Jesus, his fundamental message of forgiveness, and that was the cause of Satan's falling. When you take away the sin, you necessarily take away the power of the Accuser.

V11 "They have conquered him by the blood of the Lamb and by the word of their testimony."

"By the blood of the Lamb", of course, means "through the fact that Jesus died and was raised from the dead", referring to the language of ch5. Forgiveness becomes available because the Lamb of God "takes away the sin of the world" (John ch1 v29). So the brethren have conquered the Accuser, destroying his power over their own lives, by accepting the offered forgiveness. They have also conquered and are conquering him "by the word of their testimony". That is, they've been destroying his power over others by spreading the gospel of forgiveness, even if it brought danger to themselves, "for they loved not their lives even unto death."

The real meaning of the "battle in heaven", then, is what happened on the Cross. And the real meaning of the "fall from heaven" is that forgiveness became available because of what happened on the Cross. This was how "the salvation and the power and the kingdom" of God and his Christ came into the world.

So the story of the battle in heaven and the "Great Fall" is really nothing more- and nothing less- than a dramatized version of the doctrine of the Atonement. As we've already learned from the fifth chapter, the Atonement is the driving force at the heart of Revelation, just as it is the driving force of the rest of the New Testament.

Incidentally, I must be fair to Milton here. I was tempted to remark on the difference between this interpretation and the "battle in heaven and fall" described in Paradise Lost. But when I look closely, I see that he distinguishes between that "pre-Creation" story and the events of this chapter;

"O for that warning voice, which he who saw

The Apocalypse heard cry in Heaven aloud,

Then when the dragon put to *second* rout

Came furious down to be revenged on men"- Book IV 111-4 (my italics)

V12 "Rejoice, the O heaven and you that dwell therein! But woe to you O earth and sea!"

This is a partial fulfilment of the psalm; "Let the heavens be glad, and let the earth rejoice; let the sea roar, and all that fills it" Psalm 96 v11). The Psalm refers to the time when the Lord comes "to judge the world with righteousness". In this verse, the heavens are rejoicing already because of the downfall of Satan, but the other two regions of the created world are still in trouble.

*"The devil has come down to you in great wrath, because he knows that his time is short."*

Precisely because the real source of his power has been destroyed, he comes down upon them now with all the proverbial ferocity of the mortally wounded animal. He pursues the woman as a way of striking back at the Christ who inflicted the mortal wound in the first place. This is a key point in the explanation, as the church now learns the real reason for the tribulation suffering. The persecution is Satan's revenge for the Atonement. The logic is; "I am still the Accuser. If I can't accuse them before God, I shall accuse them before the Roman authorities."

V14 "The woman was given the two wings of the great eagle that she might fly from the serpent into the wilderness."

The imagery of this episode is deliberately echoing the Exodus of Israel from Egypt. Both episodes are in flight from a hostile power. Pharaoh has been described as "the great dragon that lies in the midst of his streams" (Ezekiel ch29 v3). The image of this verse has been inspired by the words of the Lord at Sinai; "You have seen what I did to the Egyptians, and how

I lifted you up on eagles' wings and brought you to myself" (Exodus ch19 v4).

V15 "The serpent poured water like a river out of his mouth after the woman, to sweep her away with the flood."

"Egypt rises like the Nile, like rivers whose waters surge. He said, I will rise, I will cover the earth, I will destroy cities and their inhabitants" (Jeremiah ch46 v8).

V16 "The earth opened its mouth and swallowed the river."

"Thou didst stretch out thy right hand, the earth swallowed them"(Exodus ch15 v12).

The final similarity, of course, is the culmination of both episodes in a successful escape into the wilderness, where the people will be "nourished" by their God.

There's a clear message in these parallels; that God's people should be expecting to be oppressed- perhaps to the point of possible extinction- by hostility in a place of power, as at the time of the Exodus. But that God himself will be able to preserve it by his own power- as at the time of the Exodus. It goes "underground", as we would say nowadays. The persecuting power cannot grasp the church as a body, and can only seize upon the individuals who attract its attention ("the rest of her offspring").

However, there's another angle which may be worth considering. Hosea contains a complaint, from the Lord, that his people Israel- his "wife"- have not been faithful to him in the land which he gave them. They've been learning corruption, and injustice, and idolatry. he proposes, therefore, to take their comforts away from them; "I will put an end to all her mirth, her new moons, and all her appointed feasts". And then he plans to take her into the wilderness, in order to complete the cleansing process, and to make it possible to renew the relationship; "And there she shall answer as in the days of her youth, as at the time when she came out of the land of Egypt" (Hosea ch2 vv11-15).

There is the possibility that something similar could be happening when the "woman" in this chapter is "taken into the wilderness". She too might have developed corrupt and idolatrous ways. She too, perhaps, might benefit from an experience which would take her away from her comforts and temptations, and force her to focus once more on the essence of her relationship with God. But the final purpose od the exercise proposed in Hosea was the restoration of Israel. Just as the final purpose of the original wilderness experience was that it was a time of preparation for their entrance into the Promised land.

*"And he stood on the sand of the sea."*

"Other authorities" read "I stood". Both versions are setting up the vision of the next chapter, where the Beast from the sea appears, apparently summoned by the dragon, in order to be the instrument of "making war".

# 12

# THE BEAST

## (Revelation Chapter 13)

In fact there are two Beasts in this chapter, namely the Beast from the sea and the Beast from the land. Together with the dragon, which came down from the heavens, they cover between them Revelation's three regions of the created world.

The Beast from the sea is clearly modelled on the beasts which came up out of the sea in Daniel ch7. At least three of these can be identified as imperial powers. There was the iconic winged lion of Babylon, the lopsided bear which represents the coalition of Medes and Persians, and the winged leopard representing the fast-moving empire of Alexander. Those details are echoed in the information that this beast has a lion's mouth and bear's feet, and is "like a leopard" in some unspecified way. On that analogy, we must assume that the Beast from the sea represents imperial power. That must be our starting-point.

V1 "I saw a beast rising out of the sea, with ten horns and seven heads and ten diadems upon its horns."

The basic shape of this beast is the shape of the dragon. They are like father and son. The only difference is the bizarre-looking transfer of the diadems from the heads to the ten horns. This may be anticipating the "ten kings" episode of ch17. As before, "ten" indicates the world-wide extension of their power,

As before, again, "seven" indicates that the heads are ultimately under God's control, which works in several ways. In the first place, Paul points out that there is "no authority except from God, and those that exist have been instituted by God" (Romans ch13 v1). Authorities normally act as his agents in suppressing crime and providing justice for the benefit of the world at large.

This doesn't necessarily cease to be the case even when they're acting directly against God's people. The prophets claimed that the Babylonians were unconsciously acting as God's agents in the capture of Jerusalem and the exile of the Jews. Even as outright enemies, in any case, they must fall under his limitation. Their power and authority, although ostensibly given them by the dragon, is only possible to the extent that God is willing to allow it.

*"And a blasphemous name upon its heads."*

So the dominating political power thinks it's God? Yes, that rather goes with the territory. There is a reason why absolute monarchies are called "absolute". There is a reason why totalitarian states are called "totalitarian". Political power tends towards making its claim to obedience more and more unconditional, until the point is reached where it encroaches on the claim that belongs to God.

If each of the heads thinks it's God, that might suggest that they dominate the world one at a time. in other words, they appear in succession rather than simultaneously. We may observe that the "haughty and blasphemous words" of v5 are only coming from one mouth. They are called "seven kings" in ch17, but for the purposes of this chapter it is probably better to regard them as successive imperial powers like the beasts in Daniel.

V3 "One of the heads seemed to have a mortal wound, but its mortal wound was healed."

This is easy enough to understand if the "head" is taken as representing an imperial power. I've seen one such mortal wound in my own lifetime, with the collapse of the Soviet empire and the dismantling of the Soviet Union itself. It's also possible to detect, in Putin, the beginnings of the "healing" and recovery. Other examples in modern history include the mortal wounds inflicted by revolution on Tsarist Russia (healed by Stalin), and Imperial China (healed by Mao-tse-Tung).

*"The whole earth followed the beast with wonder."*

The head is healed, and the wonder is attached to the Beast, as though the "wounded head" and the Beast are the same thing. This seems to confirm that the heads are coming in succession. Each head in turn must be the current manifestation of the Beast for its own time, and the "wounded head" would be the seventh and last in the series. There isn't likely to be much value, though, in trying to identify the symbolic number of heads with specific states in world history.

V4 "They worshipped the beast, saying 'Who is like the beast, and who can fight against it?'"

My theory of the structure of Revelation is that the world-dominating state of this chapter is the natural product of the first world-collapse in ch6. That is, the mortal wound is the general breakdown inflicted by the experience of the Four Horsemen episode. The "seventh-head" power collapses, or even disintegrates, under the impact, and so does the rest of the world. But the seventh head itself makes a vigorous recovery, so that social order comes back to life with remarkable speed. The world reacts with astonishment, but also with enthusiasm, because the recovery of the "head" is pulling the rest of the world along with it and brings it back to life.

V7 "And authority was given it over every tribe and people and tongue and nation, and all who dwell on earth will worship it."

This would follow on from the above. Naturally much of the authority would be exercised indirectly, through the rulers of client-states, as implied by the submission of the "ten kings" (ch17 v13).

The second Beast, the Beast from the land, is a man who talks. He provides "the mouth uttering haughty and blasphemous words against God (vv4-5). In later chapters, this character is being called "the false prophet", and the word "beast" tends to refer to the first Beast, the imperial state.

V11 "The I saw another beast which rose out of the earth; it had two horns like a lamb, and it spoke like a dragon."

The horns ought to be a good thing, because they seem to identify the speaker with Christ, the Lamb of God. However, the actual content of his speech gives him away. The spirit that motivates him is not the spirit of Christ.

This looks to be one of the many "false Christs" who will lead people astray, according to the warnings of Jesus (Matthew ch24 vv23-26). In principle, they should be easy to spot. The advice, in summary, is that anyone claiming to be the returned Christ while visibly present on earth, so that people can go and see him, must be a fake. A "reincarnation of Jesus"? Yes, that's a fake. That's not how Christ will return.

The speaker also fits the probable definition of John's word "antichrist" (1 John ch2 v18). The basic meaning of the Greek preposition ANTI is "standing over against". This can have a neutral meaning, as where the Lebanon mountain range stands opposite the Anti-Lebanon. It can denote a replacement, substitute or rival, and of course it overlaps with the concept of "hostility". If the speaker is a false Christ and therefore an antichrist, then he must be the last and greatest of them all. That would justify the popular term "*The* Antichrist".

However, the word doesn't appear in the book of Revelation itself, so I'll refrain from adopting it here. Indeed I must admit I don't like using the label, because it carries so many associations from mediaeval fantasy and Hollywood fantasy and other speculations. All this baggage tends to confuse discussion of the figure found in Revelation.

V12 "It exercises all the authority of the first beast in its presence."

If the first Beast is an imperial state of some kind and the second Beast is a man, then the simplest way to understand the relationship between the two is by the premise that the man is the human leader of that state. On that assumption, everything falls into place. The Empire cannot act in person, because the Empire is not a person. The Empire, as such, cannot hold meetings with generals, or dictate letters to secretaries, or shout at incompetent subordinates and threaten to dismiss them. All these things, the practical exercise of authority, demand the intervention of a human individual. That is how the Emperor "exercises the authority of the Empire in its presence".

*"It makes the earth and its inhabitants worship the first beast, whose mortal wound was healed."*

Thus confirming that the mortal wound was the experience of the corporate state, not the human individual.

Arnold Toynbee, in "A Study of History", and in other places, draws attention to a form of political religion which he calls "collective self-worship", when a society becomes its own god. As when Vespasian instituted the worship of the GENIUS POPULI ROMANI ("the spirit of the Roman people"). He finds it in the city-state loyalties of ancient Greece, and the nationalism of modern Europe.

Toynbee foresees that this might be enlarged into a "collective worship of Humanity". I've already suggested that the first Beast, the world-state, would rise to power on the strength of leading the world into recovery from the great catastrophe. In those circumstances, the population of the world would easily recognise the world-state as a projection of themselves, and the state's leader would be encouraging them to do so. "Collective self-worship" would be the natural result, and there would be no need for compulsion- when did people ever need compulsion to worship themselves?

V13 "It works great signs, even making fire come down from heaven to earth in the sight of men."

This, again, is about the promotion of worship. It imitates the story in which Elijah called down the fire to vindicate his God against the prophets of Baal (1 Kings ch18). The implication is that the Beast would appear to reverse the issue of the Mt. Carmel episode, by scattering the power of the Christian church.

V14 "Bidding them make an image for the beast that was wounded by the sword and yet lived."

I'm going to propose Adolf Hitler as the model for this verse. I'm told that the Hitler analogy is getting overdone, but it can't be helped. The relationship between Adolf Hitler and his nation is the best possible illustration of the way this might work. The starting-point is the "mortal wound" which Imperial Germany received as a consequence of the First

World War. Hitler's first aim and achievement was the perceived recovery from that wound, renewing the state's ability to project power over neighbouring countries. Meanwhile, at the Nuremberg rallies and elsewhere, he was using sight and sound to build an image of the glory of the German Volk. In effect, he was inviting his German audience to worship themselves, collectively. He caused this image to speak by being the spokesman- he could have borrowed Churchill's phrase and said that he "provided the roar".

In the event, the worship demanded by the Beast develops a double focus. It is part of our human nature that we focus our attention more easily on the visible and concrete, which is why we are prone to idolatry. So the worship is focussed on the second Beast, the visible human, as representing the first. The Roman authorities began testing Christian loyalty to the Empire by demanding the offering of incense "to the Emperor". For that matter, the Nazi adoration of the Volk was notoriously combined with the adoration of Hitler himself. In the words of a German decree of 1933, "Anyone not wishing to come under suspicion of behaving in a consciously negative manner will therefore render the "Hitler greeting" (i.e. the Nazi salute).

This brings us to the question of the Mark.

V16 "It causes all... to be marked on the right hand or the forehead."

This is how the Beast claims and brands his servants, the direct counterpart of the way that God marks his own servants (ch7). So we may take it that those who don't accept the Mark are those who have already accepted the seal, their spiritual protection.

At the same time, we should see in the background the commands of Deuteronomy; "These words which I command you this day shall be upon your heart; and you shall teach them diligently to your children, and shall talk of them when you sit in your house... And you shall bind them as a sign upon your hand, and they shall be as frontlets before your eyes" (Deuteronomy ch6 vv6-8). Those last words were not meant to be taken literally. The Pharisees took them literally and duly bound phylacteries with scripture texts in the appointed places, but that just shows how pedantic literalism can be an excellent way of missing the point. The essence of the passage as a whole is that God's law should be at the forefront of their *minds*.

In that case, it is not necessary to assume that the Mark is literally placed on hand or forehead. The meaning is that God's law has been displaced in their minds by the Beast's law, or rather by his "lawlessness". It is tempting to suppose that the Mark might be purely spiritual, just as the seal is spiritual. However, we see in the next verse that failure to accept the Mark has social consequences. That could only be possible if people could see at least a visible manifestation of the Mark, like the offering of incense in the Roman persecutions, or some equivalent, in a future tribulation, of the "Hitler greeting" and swastika of the Nazi era.

V17 "So that no one can buy or sell unless he has the mark."

In other words they will be boycotted as a punishment for stubbornly isolating themselves from what the community at large has chosen to do. Boycotting is the classic first weapon that a majority can use against a minority (the Nazis used it against the Jews). The "social credit system" being developed in China looks like an ideal tool for the purpose.

V18 "Let him who has understanding reckon the number of the beast, for it is a human number, its number is six hundred and sixty-six."

Literally, "number of a man". The New International Version (at least in the older edition on my bookshelves) used to offer the translation "is man's number". That can't have been quite right, because "man", the collective noun, is a modern English idiom. A Greek of John's time, meaning the whole species, would surely have written "men". Yet "human number", "the kind of number which would attach to a man", is probably closer to John's meaning than "the number of a specific man".

Our first clue is the symbolic meaning of number. In the Genesis story of Creation, humanity appeared on the sixth day, which means that "6" points us towards humanity almost as clearly as "7" points us towards God. In the false worship just described, adoration of a man is combined with adoration of a human institution. Either way, something human is at the centre of worship. This is an evil, not because humanity is evil, but because humanity is not God. Idolatry is the act of setting up not-God in the place which belongs to the Creator God. The raising of humanity itself to the place of God is that ultimate idolatry which goes right back to the Tower of Babel.

There may be further symbolism in the fact that 666 was King Solomon's annual income in golden talents (1 Kings ch10 v14). For we learn in the next chapter of Kings that Solomon was an idolater. He loved many foreign women and his wives turned his heart after many gods, so that his heart was not wholly true to the Lord his God. The coincidence of "666" could be taken as a hint that the great ruler of this chapter would be another multiple idolater.

At the same time, we must not disregard the instruction to "calculate" the number, which looks like a clear reference to the techniques of Gematria. Representing numbers by letters of the alphabet was a standard practice in John's time. Gematria reversed the process, by taking a name, turning the letters into numbers, and calculating a total.

As regards the message for the church of John's time, many scholars think that "666" could have been reached by calculating from the letters of Nero's name. I don't see that we need to look much further for a principal solution. I've seen the suggestion that the alternative "616", found in one papyrus, was based on working from the Latin version of his name. However, Nero belongs to the "present" tribulation of the first chapter. The narrative sequence of Revelation puts a distance between the "present" tribulation and the future Beast. So the Beast is not Nero himself, but formed in the same mould. That is, someone with a high opinion of himself, who kills many Christians. Diocletian, for example, would fit the bill.

Looking among modern names for a modern version of the calculation is a fruitless exercise, for a number of reasons which I will defer to a later page. If we want to apply this verse to some future tribulation, we should be content with the same conclusion that John's church would have reached; "Nero in the first instance, and later another despot of the same type".

Having got this far, we should go back and pick up what this chapter says about "the war on the saints". This is the same war that was covered from the viewpoint of the Two Witnesses in ch11, so these two "flashback" chapters have nearly caught up with the main sequence of Revelation. The Mark makes it easy for the Beast to identify those who resist his claims. We're told that he's allowed to make war on the saints and to conquer them (v7).

That last phrase should not be misunderstood. He may be able to seize their bodies and drive the community out of public life, but this does not mean that he can conquer their faith. As was promised in ch11, the nations can enter the "outer courts" of the Temple, but not the inner sanctum. Once the faithful have disappeared from view, the Beast is worshipped by the remainder, those whose names have not been recorded in the Lamb's book of life.

Four important statements then follow, for the benefit of the suffering faithful.

V9 "If anyone has an ear, let him hear."

That instruction can be found in the gospels, attached to the parable of the Sower, which is interesting. It may be a warning to the believers facing this crisis, not to become those who "when tribulation or persecution arise because of the word, immediately they fall away" (Mark ch4 v17).

It's also a refrain to the "letters to the seven churches", so it's now picking up the two messages of those letters (as already discussed). On the one hand, the churches being warned about the twin dangers of persecution and spiritual seduction. On the other hand, the promise of eternal life for those who can conquer the dangers.

V10 "If anyone is to be taken captive, to captivity he goes."

This comes from Jeremiah's version of the Four Fates awaiting the inhabitants of Jerusalem at the hands of the Babylonians (Jeremiah ch15 v2). The point of his message was that their immediate fate would be inescapable. On the other hand, we all know that this Exile was followed by the Return and the rebuilding of the city and temple. So anything that reminds us about the fate of Jerusalem also reminds us of the end of the story.

*"If anyone slays with the sword, with the sword he must be slain."*

At first glance, this looks like another echo of the Jeremiah verse; "And those who are for the sword, to the sword". But it's really quoting the rebuke made by Jesus in the garden of Gethsemane, in the arrest scene; "All who take the sword will perish by the sword" (Matthew ch26 v52). In effect, he was telling the disciples "This is going to happen, you can't fight it." That is the same point that Jeremiah was making, and, again, we know the end of the story. We know that the arrest and the Crucifixion were followed by the Resurrection.

*"Here is a call for the endurance and the faith of the saints."*

That is the keynote of the book of Revelation, the reason why the book was written. The previous three statements all carry the same message; "There is trouble close at hand, and in the immediate future the trouble may be inescapable. Nevertheless, there is the promise of Life on the other side of the trouble." Those who believe in this promise are those who will be able to "overcome".

# 13

# THE HERALD ANGELS

## (Revelation Chapter 14)

V1 "On Mount Zion stood the Lamb, and with him a hundred and forty-four thousand who had his name and his Father's name written on their foreheads."

There are two different ways of taking this new scene. On the one hand, it is the climax of the account of the Beast. These are the faithful number "sealed" in the seventh chapter. One of the signs of their sealing is that they have God's name marked on their foreheads instead of the name of the Beast. This is their state of presence in heaven, and many of them (not necessarily all of them) will have been martyred already.

V3 "They sing a new song before the throne and before the four living creatures and before the elders."

At the same time, on the other hand, they are resuming the interrupted heavenly response to the blowing of the seventh trumpet in ch11. They follow on from the praise of the twenty-four elders. After the two "flashback" chapters, we are returning to the main sequence of the events of Revelation.

Isaiah and the Psalms are also offering " a new song". "Sing to the Lord a new song" comes in the middle of the Servant Songs, and is followed by the promise that the Lord will lead his people out of Babylon. Psalm 96 begins in the same way, with praise about the glory and strength of God, and ends with the proclamation that the Lord is coming to "judge the world with righteousness, and the peoples with his truth" (Psalm 96 v13).

*"No one could learn that song except the hundred and forty-four thousand who had been redeemed from the earth."*

The best explanation of this constraint is to be found in Paul; "The unspiritual man does not receive the gifts of the Spirit of God, for they are folly to him, and he is not able to understand them because they are spiritually discerned" (1 Corinthians ch2 v14).

V4 "It is these who have not defiled themselves with women, for they are chaste."

The ultra-literal reading of this verse has earned the mockery of the satirist. The statement should be understood as a metaphor about spiritual fidelity, a counterpart of the "fornication" of the Harlot of Babylon as a metaphor about spiritual infidelity. They are not literally a company of bachelors, any more than they are literally one hundred and forty-four members of the tribes of Israel. They are the complete assembly of God's faithful people, whether single or married, male or female. Being found faithful to the Lamb, they are allowed to follow him wherever he goes.

V5 "And in their mouth no lie was found."

We may compare; "Those who are left in Israel, they shall do no wrong and utter no lies, neither shall there be found in their mouth a deceitful tongue" (Zephaniah ch3 v13).

V6 "Then I saw another angel flying in midheaven, with an eternal gospel to proclaim to those who dwell on earth."

He is called "another" because he follows the angels with trumpets. The fresh angels of this chapter have been sent to explain the significance of the sounding of the seventh trumpet. His message is addressed to "every nation and tribe and tongue and people", which also defines (ch13 v7) the kingdom under the sway of the Beast. The announcement of judgement is a gospel because the removal of the old world is "good news" for the victims of the old world. It is "eternal" as part of God's eternal word, never ceasing to be valid. This is not, in principle, different from the gospel found in the rest of the New Testament, which is also based on the imminence of judgement.

V7 "Fear God and give him the glory, for the hour of his judgement has come."

This repeats the warning of the "mighty angel" of ch10, before the trumpet was sounded. The approach of judgement is given as a reason for fearing and worshipping God as the one who made the different parts of the world. The two themes go together, because judgement is about putting right the world God made, making the world more complete.

V8 "Another angel, a second, followed, saying 'Fallen is Babylon the great'".

This proclamation follows on logically from the announcement that the hour of judgement has come. This verse anticipates the later description. Babylon has not yet been introduced as a character, though the church would have recognised their private nickname for Rome (as in, probably, 1 Peter ch5 v13)

The two scenes at the end of the chapter may as well be brought into this part of the discussion. They go back to the proclamation of God's judgement against the nations, found in the prophet Joel; "Put in the sickle, for the harvest is ripe. Go and tread, for the wine-press is full, the vat overflows, for their wickedness is great"- Joel ch3 v13. These two metaphors- the time of the wheat harvest and the time of the wine-harvest- are now developed into little dramas which John can witness.

V14 "Seated on the cloud, one like a son of man… a sharp sickle in his hand."

V15 "Put in your sickle and reap, for the hour to reap has come, for the harvest is fully ripe."

Both scenes contain a figure associated with "judging the world" in other parts of the Bible. In this first scene, the "one like a son of man" comes from Daniel ch7

V18 "The angel who has power over fire… 'Put in your sickle and gather the clusters of the vine of the earth, for its grapes are ripe.'"

This figure, in the second scene, appears to be the same angel who launches the "seven trumpets" at the beginning of ch8, by throwing fire from the altar upon the earth.

The remarkable depth and breadth of the overflow of the wine-press needs to be looked at more closely. "Sixteen hundred stadia", as a literal distance, would be about two hundred miles. Perhaps, once more, we should be looking for the symbolic meaning. "1600" can be broken down into the combination "4x4x10x10". That is, we find the symbolism of the number "10", which points us towards "completeness", and also the four directions. So I'm inclined to understand the distance as indicating "the fullness of the world in all directions". In Joel, it should be remembered, the overflowing is ultimately a measure of the *wickedness* of the world's population.

In other words, these two scenes are not new "events" in the storyline of Revelation. They're simply additional, metaphorical ways of expressing the message of the first two proclamations- that the hour of judgement has come, and the old world is going to be overthrown.

Vv9-10 "If anyone worships the beast and its image and receives a mark… he also shall receive the wine of God's wrath."

The central message of the third angel's proclamation is the need to avoid any association with the Beast. Once again, this is the logical consequence of the proclamation that the hour of judgement has come, for the Beast is going to be judged..

As always in Revelation, there's the question of how literally the language of "eternal torture, and the denial of rest" is meant to be understood. But the essence of the message doesn't depend on literal interpretation. The point is that receiving the Mark, which indicates loyalty to the Beast, is understood by God as a decision against himself. It is a serious business, with serious consequences.

V12 "Here is a call for the endurance of the saints."

The logic is that knowing what happens to the followers of the Beast should be motivating the saints to resist the pressure to compromise their faith and attach themselves to the doomed regime.

V13 "Blessed are the dead who die in the Lord henceforth".

The voice from heaven gives the positive side of the third angel's proclamation. This relates, in the first instance, to those who have resisted the Beast and carried their resistance to the point of martyrdom. Instead of losing from their resistance, they have gained "rest".

What does "henceforth" mean? When does the blessing begin? At first glance, the obvious meaning would be "as from this point in the narrative". But that point in the narrative is rather late in the story for the blessing to convey much benefit. Surely we must bring back the word "henceforth" at least to the moment when John hears the voice and the message is published in Revelation, to cover the martyrs of John's own time and onwards. Or rather, indeed, to the moment when Christ rose from the dead, and it first became possible to die "in the Lord", and gain from the power of his resurrection. There is perhaps no need to restrict the benefit of the blessing to the martyrs themselves. It is part of a promise which belongs to the church at large; "For whoever enters God's rest also ceases from his labours as God did from his"(Hebrews ch4 v10).

*Stephen Disraeli*

# 14

# THE CLIMAX

## (Revelation Chapters 15&16)

V1 "The seven plagues, which are the last, for with them the wrath of God is ended."

Just as the opening of the seventh seal revealed the seven trumpets, so now the sounding of the seventh trumpet announces the seven bowls of plague. We were warned, at the end of ch8, to expect three "woes" from the last three trumpets. We will find that the seven plagues between them, constitute the last of these woes.

V2 "I saw what appeared to be a sea of glass mingled with fire."

The fire of judgement on earth is visible through the transparent crystal firmament, which has been John's vantage point since the fourth chapter. "Those who have conquered the beast" (the choir of saints from the previous chapter) now resume their praise.

V3 "And they sing the song of Moses and the song of the Lamb."

The song of Moses (or Miriam) was a celebration of the destruction of Pharaoh. In the Exodus event, God was overcoming the oppressor and preparing the way for a new covenant relationship; "Thou hast led in thy steadfast love the people whom thou hast redeemed… wilt bring them in and plant them on thy own mountain, the place, O Lord, which thou hast made for thy abode (Exodus ch15 v13, v17). The song of the Lamb is the same kind of celebration in the same kind of context. God alone is holy and to be feared, because he brings justice and truth.

The sixteenth chapter is devoted to a description of the seven bowls. This is the climax of the catastrophe process which commenced in the eighth chapter, and each bowl (where appropriate) brings the climax to the operation of the corresponding trumpet.

Thus the first trumpet was an "Exodus" indicator, bringing one of the plagues of Moses, and so is the first bowl. Specifically, the "foul and evil sores" echo the boils and sores of Exodus ch9 v10. Thus confirming the message that these events are about the redemption of God's people from oppression.

The effect of the second trumpet was that a third of the sea became blood, and a third of its living creatures died. The effect of the second bowl is that the whole sea, presumably, becomes "like the blood of a dead man". I once asked a medical friend what the blood of a dead man would be like, and the suggestion was "black and crusty". So the state of the sea suffers a catastrophic degradation, and the result, not surprisingly, is that "every living thing died that was in the sea".

The effect of the third trumpet touched a third of the rivers and fountains, with the result that their waters became bitter and poisonous. The effect of the third bowl, like the effect of the second bowl, takes the degradation a stage further, so that all the land-based waters "became blood".

The effect of the fourth trumpet was that the sun and the moon and the stars lost a third of their light. This implies that the light was being blocked by some kind of pollution in the atmosphere. The effect of the fourth bowl, on the other hand, is that the sun is "allowed to scorch men with fire". One wonders if this could refer to a depletion of the ozone layer.

That is the impact on the physical environment of the human race.

The effect of the fifth trumpet was that the human race was plunged into intense despair. It was the kind of despair which would be felt by someone who was being denied even the escape-route of death. I've already shown how this echoes one of the complaints of Job. The effect of the fifth bowl is that the kingdom of the Beast is plunged into "darkness". Given that the sun is currently "scorching men with fire", I take this to be a spiritual or psychological darkness, in keeping with the fifth trumpet. We're told that men "cursed the God of heaven for their pains and sores". In this, they're following the advice which Job received from his wife, when he was suffering from his own "loathsome sores" ("curse God and die"-Job ch2 v9).

This appears to indicate that the population of the world is undergoing a collective "Job" experience. Their physical world is falling apart, just as Job's world fell apart around him, The loss of hope in the future, the abandonment of faith, would be a very natural consequence. So that is the impact on the psychological environment of the human race.

The effect of the sixth trumpet was that the world was invaded by forces which came from the Euphrates. The effect of the sixth bowl is the gathering together of the kings of the world, but at least some of them are coming from the east, from the other side of the Euphrates. The waters of the Euphrates are dried up, which serves a double purpose. It symbolises the fulfilment of the prophet's warning to Babylon, that her waters would be "dried up", that her power would be drained away, in the time of her destruction (Jeremiah ch50 v38). That's in addition to the practical purpose, of making it easier for the kings of the east to cross over.

As far as I'm concerned (as previously discussed), "coming across the Euphrates" should be seen as a symbolic act. That river counts as the boundary between the ordered civilised world and the world "outside". The impact of the sixth trumpet and the sixth bowl is upon the social environment of the human race.

V13 "I saw issuing from the mouth of the dragon and from the mouth of the beast and from the mouth of the false prophet, three foul spirits."

Given that "false prophet" is another name for the "Beast from the land", these three figures between them were responsible for the persecution of the church in ch13. We should, then, suspect that further persecution is on the way.

V14 "[The spirits] go abroad to the kings of the whole world, to assemble them for battle on the great day of God the Almighty."

The ostensible effect, in the vision, is the summoning of the rulers of earth to a battle. We should see Joel in the background of this image; "Let the men of war draw near, let them come up... Let the nations bestir themselves and come up to the valley of Jehoshaphat; For there I will sit to judge all the nations round about... For the Day of the Lord is near, in the valley of decision" (Joel ch3 vv9-14). For centuries, God had been fighting off the enemies of his people among the nations. In that prophecy, he gets rid of the problem by gathering together all the enemies and potential enemies in one place, and vanquishing them, once and for all. After that, no more enemies.

In this chapter, God's enemies are unaware that the summons comes from God. They think they are summoning themselves. Nevertheless, the summons has the same ultimate purpose. The nations are coming together so that God can judge them.


V15 "Lo, I am coming like a thief. Blessed is he who keeps awake, keeping his garments that he may not go naked and be seen exposed."

This interjection must be taken as the direct words of Christ. The parallels in other parts of the New Testament show that "coming like a thief" means coming suddenly, without warning. Thus; "The day of the Lord will come like a thief, and the heavens will pass away with a loud noise" (1 Peter ch3 v10).

Paul refers to the necessity of keeping awake; "The day of the Lord will come like a thief in the night...sudden destruction will come upon them...so then, let us not sleep, as others do, but let us keep awake and be sober" (1 Thessalonians ch5 vv2-6). The reference in the gospels is more oblique; "If the householder had known in what part of the night the thief was coming, he would have watched..." (Matthew ch24 v41). It's evident, though, that the theme goes back to the words of Jesus, associated with the expectation of his return. And this return of Christ, like the "day of the Lord" in the Old Testament, is expected (as Paul testifies) to include the act of judgement. To be "awake", then, means keeping oneself in a state of preparation for judgement.

"Keeping his garments" can be part of the "keeping awake" theme; the man who doesn't go to bed is not going to disrobe, to avoid being caught naked when the alarm bell sounds. However, there's also a spiritual metaphor which goes back to the story of Adam and Eve. They were "naked and exposed" because their sin was visible in the sight of God. They tried to cover themselves, but the more effective solution was the clothing which God provided. For the New Testament, the answer is to be "clothed in Christ", as Paul puts it (Galatians ch3 v27). The church of Laodicea was advised to acquire "white garments" from Christ, "to keep the shame of your nakedness from being seen" (ch3 v18). In fact this white robe, which represents redemption from sin, is the standard garment for the servants of God in Revelation. So there is the garment which must cover our nakedness in the time of judgement.

V16 "They assembled them at the place which is called in Hebrew Armageddon."

The key to understanding this battle is to appreciate that Armageddon is the re-running of the battle of Megiddo (609 B.C.) Megiddo is the battle in which God's champion, Josiah, stood up against the enemies of God and was defeated, a result which cannot be allowed to stand.

Josiah was very much the Lord's king. It was during his reign that the "book of the Law", commonly identified as Deuteronomy, was "discovered" by the priests of the Temple. Josiah took steps to proclaim the Law, and to renew the nation's covenant with the Lord. He made a point of removing anything that might be considered idolatrous from the territories under his control. He was the king who abolished the provincial altars of Yahweh, and centralised the worship and the celebration of the Passover at Jerusalem. "Before him, there was no king like him, who turned to the Lord with all his heart and with all his soul and with all his might, according to the law of Moses, nor did any like him arise after him." ( 2 Kings ch23 v25).

This achievement was thrown away in one moment of madness. The Pharaoh Necho was on his way to fight great wars further to the north. Josiah chose to intercept him, at Megiddo, and lost his life. The ultimate sequel, and perhaps the consequence, was the destruction of his kingdom at the hands of the king of Babylon. The loss of Josiah was deeply mourned. The "laments" which were written around the event were still sung centuries later- "to this day", as the Chronicler puts it. Much hope must have been invested in this king, by those who followed the Lord. The disappointment of the battle would surely compare with the sense of loss of the disciples on the road to Emmaus; "We had hoped that he was the one to redeem Israel". In effect, the death of Josiah was the Good Friday of the Old Testament period.

I believe that the resemblance between these two battles should be sought not in the location, but in the parallel between the two sets of combatants. In the one corner, ladies and gentlemen, God's anointed king, the champion of God's people. In the other corner, the power of oppression, as represented by the Egyptians, and by the "kings of the earth". The first time this battle was fought, at Megiddo, the result was a catastrophe. Therefore the same battle must be fought all over again, at Armageddon, so that the result can be reversed. It would symbolise, at the same time, the reversal of all the other apparent setbacks, from the fall of man to the supremacy of the Beast in its "war on the saints". This is God having the Last Word.

We make a serious mistake when we understand Armageddon as a battle between human armies, and apply the label to world wars. It is clear in this chapter and from the parallel in Joel that the kings of the earth are not gathering to fight each other. They are gathering so that all of them together may fight and be fought by God. For this purpose, it would not be literally necessary to gather armies into any one place. He could defeat them wherever he found them. Armageddon must be a battle in a more spiritual sense.

The real clue is the point I've already noticed, that the three summoning spirits originate from dragon, beast, and false prophet, the three promoters of persecution. The implication is that the great "war against God" takes the form of a renewal of persecution. The opening of the battle of Armageddon, from the human side, is one final intensified spasm of the campaign to destroy the Two Witnesses.


V17 "The seventh angel poured his bowl into the air… 'It is done'"

The effect of the seventh trumpet was the proclamation that the end had come, reaching the last minute of the world. The effect of the seventh bowl is the proclamation that the end has come, reaching the last second. This declaration may remind us (though the wording is different) of the "It is finished!" spoken from the Cross

V19 "And God remembered great Babylon to make her drain the cup of the fury of his wrath."

This image goes back to Jeremiah. The prophet was told to take "this cup of the wine of God's wrath" and force it upon the kings of the world. "And after them the king of Babylon shall drink" (Jeremiah ch25 v26). So the end is expressed in terms of the fall of Babylon, along with all the other cities of the nations. There is an earthquake greater than any known in history, an earthquake to bring down the whole world flat.

*Stephen Disraeli*

# 15

# THE HARLOT

## (Revelation Chapter 17)

V1 "Then one of the angels who had the seven bowls came and said to me 'Come, I will show you the judgement of the great harlot who is seated upon many waters.'"

The description of the Harlot belongs to the "Bowls" period, just as the story of the Two Witnesses was embedded among the Trumpets.

The Harlot is a complex character, and a proper understanding of her requires careful analysis. It will be necessary, for the moment, to focus on what she would have meant for the church of John's time. The angel tells us later (v15) that the waters are "peoples and multitudes and nations and tongues". We can absorb that explanation without forgetting the symbolism of "the sea as the source of evil".

V2 "With the wine of whose fornication the dwellers on earth have become drunk."

In prophetic symbolism, "fornication" is a metaphor of unfaithfulness, and "getting drunk" is a metaphor about unwitting self-preparation for judgement (as in, for example, Jeremiah ch25).

V3 "I saw a woman sitting on a scarlet beast which was full of blasphemous names, and it had seven heads and ten horns."

This is the Beast from the sea. The translators rightly distinguish between the "redness" of the dragon, and the "scarlet" of this verse, but the two colours are similar enough to demonstrate the connection. In the fifth chapter, John heard about a lion, and saw the same lion pictured as a lamb. In this chapter, he's told to expect a woman sitting on many waters, and then sees a woman sitting on the Beast. If these are equivalent seats, then the Beast must also represent "peoples and multitudes and nations and tongues". This confirms the Beast as "Rome, the Empire", and implies that the Harlot must be "Rome, the city", necessarily resting on the support of the wider institution.

Their location is "in the wilderness". In other words, they are "outsiders", not part of the land that was given to Israel.

V4 "The woman was arrayed in purple and scarlet and bedecked with gold and jewels and pearls."

This is one of the complications. The Harlot appears to be Rome, but she is also "the other woman". I've already quoted, and will now quote again, the diatribe against Jerusalem which provides the model for this scene; "And you, O desolate one, what do you mean that you dress in scarlet, that you deck yourself with ornaments of gold, that you enlarge your eyes with paint? In vain you beautify yourself, your lovers despise you, they seek your life. For I heard a cry as of a woman in travail, anguish as of one bringing forth her first child..." (Jeremiah ch4 vv30-31).

As I've already observed, the "woman in heaven" in ch12 has taken over the second verse of that passage. In effect, the two women have divided the description between them. They must represent the faithful and the unfaithful Jerusalem, the faithful and the unfaithful versions of God's people. The church of John's time would probably see the Jews as the unfaithful portion of God's people, because of their refusal to accept the authority of Christ. Perhaps we should say "the Jews of the city of Rome", looking for a way to reconcile the two interpretations.

V5 "On her forehead was written a name of mystery; 'Babylon the great, mother of harlots and of earth's abominations'."

Here is another complication. What was the significance of the word "Babylon" before the association with "harlot" became familiar? Old Testament history knew Babylon as the kingdom that destroyed the Temple of Jerusalem. The power of religious oppression, then. Old Testament prophecy (e.g. Isaiah ch46) also knew Babylon as the location of many idols, which is the meaning of the word "abomination" (e.g. Deuteronomy ch27 v15). So that is temptation to idolatry.

The Harlot appears to be an amalgam of three elements. These are unfaithfulness, represented by the Jews of Rome; religious oppression, represented by the political establishment of Rome; and the seductiveness of idolatry, represented by the religious establishment of Rome.

V6 "And I saw the woman, drunk with the blood of the saints and the blood of the martyrs of Jesus."

This is the real essence of the Harlot, the reason why the Harlot matters. All three elements in the amalgam will be contributing to this bloodthirstiness. The religious establishment are demanding conformity from the Christians. The Jews of Rome have the opportunity to be informers. The political establishment will enforce the penalties incurred by the recalcitrant.

The angel offers to explain the mystery, but his explanations will need to be explained.

V8 "The beast that you saw was and is not, and is to ascend from the bottomless pit and go to perdition."

This is still the Beast from the sea, as shown by the statement (repeated from ch13) about the marvelling of the dwellers of the earth. "Is not" implies that the Beast is in the "mortal wound" stage of its lifespan in the "present" perspective. For symbolism, the sea and the bottomless pit are the same place. The word translated "perdition" is really "destruction"; it's close to the name of Apollyon, the destroyer, who led the locusts out of the bottomless pit. In other words, this empire will go back to a final "is not".

*"It was and is not and is to come".*

Here is the definition of God (ch4 v8), carefully negated in the central element. In other words, he is Non-Being by definition, the exact opposite of the Living One. This is really the character of the dragon which lies behind the Beast.

V9 "The seven heads are seven mountains on which the woman is seated."

The standard, and probably valid, assumption is that sitting on seven mountains confirms the identity of the Harlot as "Rome, the city". The objection is sometimes raised that classical Rome was on "nine hills". However, there was an ancient celebration, the SEPTIMONTIUM ("Seven-hills-festival") which came down from an earlier phase in the city's history.

V10 "They are also seven kings, five of whom are fallen, one is, the other has not yet come, and when he comes he must remain only a little while."

Any Roman citizen who saw the term "seven kings" would have been reminded of the seven legendary kings of ancient Rome, from Romulus to Tarquin the Proud. Tarquin, the seventh, was a king who remained "only a little while". That is, he was expelled, so that he did not reign for the full extent of his life.

In a sense, the republican constitution could be called the "eighth" in that sequence. Technically, the Rome of John's time had not ceased to be a republic. From Augustus onwards, the ruler was being called PRINCEPS ("the Boss"), and his power was ultimately resting on the sword. Yet his legal authority, strictly speaking, was based on the accumulation of republican offices. We might take that as the background.

In the foreground, we must see the more recent sequence of Imperial rulers. The fact that John sees this vision in a time of tribulation should be defining the sixth and current ruler as a persecuting Emperor. Sure enough, Nero is the sixth member of the Julio-Claudian dynasty, if we begin the count with Caesar himself (Julius, Augustus, Tiberius, Caligula, Claudius, and Nero).

Commentators sometimes juggle with the sequence to try to make "the eighth" coincide with Domitian (81-96 A.D.). I think this approach is ruled out by the statement "One is", which needs to be taken more seriously. If John is writing in the reign of the sixth king, then he cannot have any names in mind for the seventh and eighth rulers. They will still be in his future.

My interpretation of "remaining only a little while" is that the seventh king is that reign or regime which does not run its full course because it is interrupted by the Four Horsemen episode. Then the central message of this verse about the seven kings would be that the first tribulation is followed by the Four Horsemen, but not immediately.

V11 "As for the beast that was and is not, it is an eighth and it belongs to the seven, and it goes to perdition."

This picks up the previous reference to the beast "from the bottomless pit", which is the Beast from the sea of ch13- the collective state, not the human individual. The relation between this Beast and the seven coincides neatly with my previous proposal for the relation between the Beast and the Four Horsemen. Just to recap, the seventh regime remains "only a little while" because it appears to have been destroyed by the Four Horsemen episode, and that is what constitutes the "mortal wound". The Beast regime "belongs to the seven", because it is the recovery and re-creation of the seventh, a recovery which earns the wonder of the rest of the world.

The Beast is not called "an eighth king", but simply "an eighth". Readers of the AV, at least, may know that Noah was saved from the waters of the flood as "an eighth" (2 Peter ch2 v5). 1 Peter observes more simply that eight people were saved on the ark, which is a symbol of baptism saving through the resurrection of Christ (1 Peter ch3 v20). The early church reckoned that Christ was raised from the dead on what was effectively the eighth day of the week, the day following the seventh. The event could even be described as "the eighth day of Creation", because it completed and perfected the work of the original seven. "Wherefore also we keep the eighth day for rejoicing, in the which our Lord Jesus Christ rose from the dead, and having been manifested ascended into heaven" (Epistle of Barnabas, 15 v9). That's exactly what John was doing in the opening chapter, "on the Lord's day". In short, this Beast has been given a number clearly associated with the Resurrection of Christ, which implies an imitation of Christ.

Modern translations of 2 Peter tend to say "Noah was saved along with seven others", which has always been one of my favourite objections to paraphrase translation. A paraphrase translator who misses the point of an expression also prevents his readers from working it out for themselves.

V12 "The ten horns that you saw are ten kings."

Ten is the number of completeness. These are not literally ten kings, but the rulers of the whole world, between them.

"They are to receive authority as kings for one hour, together with the beast."

I've already shown how the "silence in heaven, when God's wrath is not operating on the world (ch8 v1) occupies the first half of this hour. Most of the rest of this book is about the troubled second "half an hour"

V13 "These are of one mind and give over their power and authority to the beast."

That is, the Beast is able to dominate the world by indirect rule, working through a network of client rulers and client states. In the same way, the power of the hostile king in Daniel is based on making "a strong covenant with many", or many strong covenants with individuals (Daniel ch9 v27). We may compare the way that Hitler was able to dominate Europe partly by means of his varied relationships with men like Mussolini, Franco, Pierre Laval, Admiral Horthy, and Vidkun Quisling.

V14 "They will make war on the Lamb and the Lamb will conquer them."

This is another version of the battle of Armageddon introduced in the previous chapter. The human side of this war would be an intensified persecution of the church. For John's first message, I propose the persecution campaign of Diocletian as the war on the Lamb, and the victories of Constantine as the Lamb's conquest.

The final part of the chapter is a paragraph on the fate of the Harlot (vv15-18). This doesn't follow in sequence, so the angel isn't intending to suggest that the horns and the Beast are attacking the Harlot after they've already been defeated in v14.

V16 "They and the beast will hate the harlot; they will make her desolate and naked, and devour her flesh and burn her up with fire."

This was predicted in Jeremiah's diatribe against the Harlot; "Your lovers despise you, they seek your life." If the Harlot is the city and the Beast is the Empire, then the implication is that the city is destroyed by the rebellion of the outlying provinces. That is indeed a good description of what happened to Imperial Rome. The eastern provinces transferred their loyalty to the new capital in Constantinople, while the western provinces were invaded by barbarians and detached themselves.

Despite my comment just above, the Empire's desertion of Rome does take place after the defeat of at least the pagan and persecuting aspect of the Empire. Rome was devastated and devoured and burned with fire by the Vandals, who sacked the city in 455 A.D. On my theory, that is the last historical event foreseen in the first message of Revelation.


V18 "And the woman you saw is the great city which has dominion over the kings of earth."

This great city is obviously Rome, in John's time, *but only in John's time*. The equivalent city would have been Paris in the eighteenth century, London in the nineteenth century, Washington in the twentieth century, and perhaps Peking in the twenty-second century. Anyone who wants to identify the Harlot of a future tribulation should not be fixing their minds on the geographical location or the name of Rome.

Rome itself was not literally Babylon, but only the equivalent of Babylon in a combination of political dominance and religious oppression. In exactly the same way, a future "great city" would not be literally Rome, but would be the equivalent of Rome in a combination of political dominance and religious oppression. The best way to identify the Harlot is to look for the symptoms and recognise them when they appear.

# 16

# BABYLON'S WAKE

## (Revelation Chapter 18)

This chapter contains a mock lament for the expected fall of Babylon, modelled on Ezekiel's gloating "lament" for the expected fall of Tyre. The text echoes and draws upon Old Testament prophecy relating to three different cities.

*The city Babylon*

The opening proclamation echoes those that were directed against the original city of Babylon. The opening proclamation, that "Babylon the great has fallen", was first heard in one of the visions of Isaiah; "Fallen, fallen, is Babylon. and all the images of her gods" (Isaiah ch21 v9). Another prophecy predicts that Babylon will never be inhabited except by satyrs and ostriches, and other wild beasts and "howling creatures"(Isaiah ch13 vv20-22), and this finds an echo in the rest of v2.

Jeremiah is another source of prophecy against Babylon. The opening words of v3 recall the way Jeremiah sums up the effects of Babylon's power; "Babylon was a golden cup in the Lord's hand, making all the earth drunk. The nations drank of her wine, therefore the nations went mad." (Jeremiah ch51 v7).

Then the "voice from heaven" takes up the story with further echoes from both prophets. "Come out of her, my people" reflects Jeremiah's "Go out of the midst of her, my people. Let every man save his life from the fierce anger of the Lord" (Jeremiah ch51 v45). The beginning of v5 recalls his previous observation that "her judgement has reached up to heaven" (Jeremiah ch51 v9). That is the only sense in which the tower of Babel had achieved its original ambition.

The voice from heaven declares that Babylon will be paid back double for her deeds, because "God has remembered her iniquities". This can be seen as an unfavourable contrast with the promise given to Jerusalem; that her own double payment means that "her iniquity has been pardoned" (Isaiah ch40 v2). The smug self-confidence which Babylon shows in v7 is another echo; "I am, and there is no-one besides me; I shall not sit as a widow, or know the loss of children" (Isaiah ch47 vv7-8).

Thus the Babylon of history is presented as a model for Revelation's Babylon, suggesting that this Babylon is also about idolatry and the exercise of political and religious power over other people.

## The city Tyre

The weeping of the kings of the earth is modelled on Ezekiel ch26, which predicts the lamentations of "the princes of the sea". In the next chapter of Ezekiel, attention turns to the merchants of the world, and to the sailors, lamenting the loss of trade and the opportunities to gain wealth. We're given a detailed description of the commerce of Tyre, which builds up into a very instructive "trade map" of Ezekiel's world. Spain or Tarshish, for example, is the place to go for any kind of metal ore. All this trade will vanish when the city has been destroyed.

Ezekiel doesn't spell out what the city of Tyre has done to deserve destruction, but there's a good summary of the charge in the words of Joel; "You have taken my silver and my gold and have carried my rich treasures into your temples. You have sold the people of Judah and Jerusalem to the Greeks, removing them far from their own border" (Joel ch3 vv5-6). Evidently Tyre was among the nations which took advantage of the vulnerability of Judah after the fall of Jerusalem, and thus partly responsible for the Dispersion of the Jewish nation through the Mediterranean world.

The middle part of this chapter follows the pattern of Ezekiel ch27 (with occasional verbal echoes like "threw dust on their heads"). That is, it describes the mourning of the merchants and sailors because of their loss of trade. The list of articles of trade is not directly copied from Ezekiel, but re-written to cover the commerce of the Roman world. The last item on the list is the one that really matters; "Slaves- that is, human souls" (v13). The resemblance between the old city of Tyre and this Babylon is that they both take captive the "souls" which belong to God and make merchandise of them. Babylon does this partly by drawing them into beliefs and practices which belong to other gods, like the sorcerers and false prophets addressed in one of Ezekiel's prophecies; "Will you hunt down souls belonging to my people and keep other souls alive for your profit?. You have profaned me among my people...by your lies to my people, who listen to lies.(Ezekiel ch13 vv18-19)

Thus Tyre is presented as a model for Revelation's Babylon, suggesting that this Babylon is about the exercise of economic power over other people, including the ability to profit from their idolatry.

## The city Jerusalem

Another angel throws a great millstone into the sea. He's imitating some of the prophets by "acting out" the opening words of his proclamation; "So shall Babylon the great city be thrown down with violence and shall be found no more" (v21). This echoes an incident in Jeremiah's mission. The prophet instructed Seraiah to read out the words of his prophecy in Babylon itself, and then throw them into the middle of the Euphrates, attached to a stone (Jeremiah ch51 v63).

At the same time, the use of a millstone also recalls the warning of Jesus to anyone causing "one of these little ones who believe in me" to stumble in their faith; "It would be better for him to have a great millstone fastened round his neck and to be drowned in the depth of the sea" (Matthew ch18 v6). The function of Babylon has been to destroy the faith of God's people, to the extent that it might be possible.

Why do I associate this incident with Jerusalem? Because the following words of the speech echo one of Jeremiah's warnings about the infidelities of Jerusalem; "I will banish from them the voice of mirth and the voice of gladness, the voice of the bridegroom and the voice of the bride, the grinding of millstones and the light of the lamp" (Jeremiah ch25 v10). The speech serves as a reminder that selfishly motivated control, economic exploitation, and even idolatry, can also be found amongst those who are nominally part of God's people.

Thus Jerusalem is presented as a model for Revelation's Babylon, suggesting that this Babylon is about disloyalty to the Creator God, disregarding his claim on the obedience of the world.

## *Bloodshed*

The last verse relates to the blood-guilt of Babylon for the deaths of saints and prophets, which is worth considering as a separate theme. It can be attached to the Jerusalem theme, because it echoes the warning given by Jesus to the Pharisees; "Therefore I send you prophets and wise men and scribes, some of whom you will kill and crucify… that upon you may come all the righteous blood shed on earth, from the blood of innocent Abel to the blood of Zechariah the son of Barachiah" (Matthew ch23 vv34-35).

However, there is one interesting difference. Compared with the words of Jesus, Revelation omits the word "righteous" before "blood". The effect of this omission is that Babylon becomes responsible for all the blood shed in human history, including deaths in war, and all the individual, personally motivated, acts of murder. Babylon has become a synonym for "violence".

In one of Zechariah's visions, the prophet is shown a woman trapped in a pot. Her name is "Iniquity" or "Wickedness", and they're taking her away to a new home to be built in the land of Shinar, which was the location of the original Babel (Zechariah ch5 vv5-11). Here is a reason, then, to consider the place of Babel in the early stages of scripture.. We see in Genesis a progression of sin which begins with the Fall, the self-will of Adam and Eve in disobedience to God. The next stage is violence, the self-will of Cain in conflict with brethren. Strictly speaking, Babel represents pride, collective self-will in rivalry with God. However, Revelation's Babylon has become collectively violent, taking on the sin of Cain. That is how Babylon may be taken as a symbol for Iniquity in general.

Therefore "the destruction of Babylon" may be nothing less than the reversal of the effect of the Fall, which would be an even more significant reason for celebration.

# 17

# GOD IN TRIUMPH

## (Revelation Chapter 19)

The time has come for the great act of salvation which will bring the persecution to an end and judge the persecutors. This event was announced at the blowing of the seventh trumpet, and at the outpouring of the seventh bowl. Now nothing remains but the anticipatory praise.

Our attention is brought back to the throne-room setting of the fourth and fifth chapters, which has been John's implied vantage point in the intervening scenes. Just as a great multitude then celebrated the Lamb's act of Atonement, so now a great multitude in heaven celebrates this new act of salvation, which is one of its consequences. In the first place, they take up the last verse of the previous chapter, the charge of shedding the blood of the saints and prophets, and rejoice that Babylon will now be judged and their blood will be avenged.

V3 "The smoke from her goes up for ever and ever."

This is borrowed from the judgement of Edom; "Night and day [the burning pitch] will not be quenched; its smoke will go up for ever" (Isaiah ch34 v10). It is a metaphor about the completeness and permanence of her downfall.

The twenty-four elders and the four living creatures add their Amen.

Vv7-8 "The marriage of the Lamb has come, and his Bride has made herself ready; it was granted to her to be clothed with fine linen, bright and pure, for the fine linen is the righteous deeds of the saints."

Of course the bride of Christ is the church; "Christ loved the church and gave himself up for her… that he might present the church to himself in splendour, without spot or wrinkle" (Ephesians ch5 vv25-27). This image of God's people as God's bride, prepared for marriage by her own bridegroom, appears in Ezekiel (ch16 vv8-14), and also in the Song of Solomon, which is a more encouraging version of the Ezekiel parable (Song of Solomon ch8 vv8-10).

V9 "The angel said to me 'Write this; Blessed are those who are invited to the marriage supper of the Lamb.'"

This is a re-writing of the gospel statement; "Blessed is he who shall eat bread in the kingdom of God" (Luke ch14 v15). The effect is to identify these two metaphors relating to the fellowship of God's people in the presence of their God.

*"And he said to me, 'These are true words of God...*
For the testimony of Jesus is the spirit of prophecy."
These two statements belong together, the first explained by the second. The point is that the Christian apostles and prophets are prompted by the same Spirit that prompted the prophets of the Old Testament, and that's how we may know that the words of the agents of Jesus are also the words of the Old Testament God.

It isn't clear which angel has been speaking. John was last addressed (in the previous chapter) by one of the angels of the bowls, but there may be a case here for assuming the angel of Jesus from the first chapter, the one "like a son of man". The point is of interest, because John is briefly confused by the status of the angel as "representative spokesman".

The common convention is that the representative speaks the words of his principal, in the first person. So the interpreter at a bilingual meeting, and the angel of the Lord, and also (less obviously) the television image of a person facing the camera. In the first example, the practice does not cause confusion. The interpreter and the statesman are sitting side by side, and nobody thinks the interpreter is threatening to declare war in his own person. There is a desire to believe in the reality of television, so it is easy to imagine a devotee tempted to kiss the screen image of a favourite film star. Even easier to imagine the shock, if the image suddenly "broke out of character" and rebuked him; "Don't do that, you idiot! I'm just a collection of electronic impulses, not the real thing."

John has a similar experience. Hearing the angel speak the words of God, he momentarily accepts him as God and falls down to worship him. Hence the rebuke; "You must not do that! I am a fellow-servant with you and your brethren who hold the testimony of Jesus" (v10). Apparently the Jehovah's Witnesses are still confused by the "representative spokesman" convention, trying to use this incident and the similar incident in the last chapter as evidence that "Jesus is only an angel." No, the correct conclusion is that Jesus *has* an angel to speak on his behalf, just as angels speak on the Lord's behalf in the Old Testament.

Why is this incident included in Revelation? Perhaps there was a growing danger that some of the "brethren who hold the testimony of Jesus", speaking the words of God on his behalf, would receive the kind of veneration that belongs to God alone. Then the rebuke of the angel would be a timely warning that they too were nothing more than fellow-servants; "What then is Apollos? What is Paul? Servants through whom you believed, as the Lord assigned to each" (1 Corinthians ch3 v5)

V11 "The I saw heaven opened, and behold, a white horse!"

As we get closer to the climax of the "salvation from tribulation", it becomes all the more necessary to be aware of the double message of Revelation. There is a double tribulation, suffered by the church of the Roman Empire and by a future church, and therefore the promise of salvation must have a double fulfilment. There will be two versions of Armageddon, two versions of God's triumph over his enemies.

I premise that the Armageddon of the first tribulation was the battle of Milvian Bridge (312 A.D.). To be exact, the human side of Armageddon was Diocletian's campaign to destroy the church. The triumphal aspect of Armageddon was the battle at the Milvian Bridge, which gave Constantine control over the western Empire, and the Edict of Milan (in the following year) which liberated the Christian church from state-sponsored persecution. The battle is associated with the legend of Constantine's vision of the Cross.

*"He who sat upon it is called Faithful and True."*

For the purposes of John's message to the later church, the triumphal figure is Christ himself, in person. Detail is piled upon detail to establish his identity. For example, he calls himself "faithful and true witness" in ch3 v14.

His eyes are like a flame of fire- the image "like a son of man" in ch1 v14.

*"Many diadems"- multiple and complete authority.*

"A name inscribed which no one knows but himself"- the one which he promises to share in ch3 v12. The name appears to be inscribed on his head, the place of authority.

He is clad in a robe dipped in blood- his own, of course. This victory would not have been possible without the fundamental victory of the Cross.

The name which other people use about him is "The Word of God" (see John ch1). Has not the angel just confirmed that the word of God is the same thing as the testimony of Jesus?

From his mouth issues a sharp sword- another detail from the son-of-man image.

He will smite the nations and rule them with a rod of iron- as does the child caught up to heaven in ch12 (both statements quoting from Psalm 2).

This is precisely what he promised when the human "armies" were being gathered together for this battle- "Behold, I am coming like a thief!" (ch16 v15)

So here is the Return of Christ. When he made his first public entry into Jerusalem, he was a king who was "humble, and mounted on an ass." (Matthew ch21 v5)., but now he's mounted as a warrior king.

He's followed by the "armies of heaven", clothed in white linen and riding on white horses of their own. They resemble the "riders from heaven" who make an appearance, on their own or in groups, in some of the stories of 2 Maccabees (which covers the wars with Antiochus Epiphanes, the original model for the Beast). For example; "They were still near Jerusalem when a rider attired in white appeared at their head, brandishing golden weapons. With one accord they all blessed the God of mercy and found themselves filled with courage..."-(2 Maccabees ch11 v8). This army has the same purpose, in coming to the aid of God's people against their enemies.

Paul refers to this event as "the day of the Lord" (2 Thessalonians ch2 v2), or "the day of Jesus Christ" (Philippians ch1 v6), or "the day of our Lord Jesus Christ" (1 Corinthians ch1 v8). These phrases are echoes of the Old Testament expectation of "the day of the Lord". On that day, God would be asserting himself in power, overcoming the resistance of the world, coming in to judge the nations and set things right. That is the significance of the gathering "in the valley of Jehoshaphat" (Joel ch3 v12), which is one of the models of Armageddon.

In the same way, the New Testament is expecting Christ to bring judgement with him when he comes, "inflicting vengeance on those who do not know God" (2 Thessalonians ch1 v8). It's not surprising, then, that the Old Testament picture of God as the warrior for justice has been merged into this vision of the rider descending from heaven. It is God, after all, who "judges and makes war in righteousness" (v11). He is "mighty in battle", followed by great armies (Psalm 24 v8). His own garment is "sprinkled with blood" (also an alternative translation of v13), because he has "trodden the wine-press" in wrath (as in v15), coming to the aid of his people (Isaiah ch63 v3). So Revelation is providing a "day of the Lord" picture, showing divine victory followed by the judgement of the world.

V19 "I saw the beast and the kings of earth with their armies."

This will not be a literal battle fought with physical weapons. We've been told that the Son of man will come "on the clouds of heaven with power and great glory" (Matthew ch24 v30). The full expression of God's presence in power would be enough in itself to disable any resisting will and all human strength. Those who are slain are slain "by the sword that issues from his mouth" (v21), that is, by the Word. Paul suggests that the transition from the old world to the new world would take place "in the twinkling of an eye" (1 Corinthians ch15 v52). The battle would be over before it began. The victory would be instantaneous.

What about the summoning of the birds of prey to deal with the expected corpses? That has been borrowed from the account of the "final battle" with Gog of the land of Magog (Ezekiel ch39), and even in Ezekiel it is a metaphor about the finality and thoroughness of the victory.

Judgement, for the moment, means that the beast and the false prophet (the two Beasts of ch13) are thrown into the lake of fire. On the subject of the lake of fire, we can observe that one of the Beasts is an Empire, and therefore not capable of "eternal suffering". It can only cease to exist. We shall have to come back to that question in the next chapter.

# 18

# THE MILLENNIUM

## (Revelation Chapter 20)

Vv1-2 "Then I saw an angel coming down from heaven… and he seized the dragon, that ancient serpent, who is the Devil and Satan, and bound him."

The key to grasping the meaning of this chapter is to understand Satan as Revelation understands him. We must put aside the different functions which have become attached to the name in popular culture, such as "tempter" and "ruler of occult powers". In Revelation, Satan is the Accuser, denouncing the sinful to God or denouncing the redeemed to the Roman authorities. When Satan is bound, therefore, he is bound *as a persecutor*. A world in which Satan has been bound will not be a miraculously ideal world, one without temptations or other troubles. It will simply be a world which is not openly attempting to destroy the Christian community.

*"Bound him for a thousand years".*

The classic explanation comes from St Augustine in the "City of God" (Book 20, ch7). He equates the binding of Satan with the "binding of the strong man", as announced by Jesus (Mark ch3 v27) and thus with the work of Jesus himself. He does hesitate between two different ways of interpreting that "one thousand". He has half a mind to take it as a literal number (which would be a mistake, we now realise, because more than a thousand years has elapsed since Augustine's time). Alternatively, John was using a symbolic number (the cube of ten), employing the number of completeness to show the fulness of time. Either way, the beginning of his thousand year kingdom is marked by the life and death of Christ and the introduction of the gospel.

I think he is mistaken about the starting-point. His explanation is not part of a full study of Revelation, and he fails to spot a difficulty in the chronology. If the act of Atonement provides the climax to the book, coming at the beginning of this chapter, then all the previous events in Revelation should be happening before the Atonement. However, this book opens in the middle of the persecution troubling the church of John's time and then looks forward to future relief. The narrative sequence in Revelation is flexible, but not quite as flexible as that.

In addition, I think he's fixed on the wrong aspect of Satan. He would be right to identify Satan as Accuser of sin, but Satan was bound in that sense in the twelfth chapter. For me, the Edict of Milan is the event which "bound" Satan as a promoter of Imperial persecution, and therefore the beginning of the Millennium.

*"After that, he must be loosed for a little while."*
That is, there will be a final tribulation following this current period of comparative peace, and then the encouraging message of Revelation will become applicable all over again.

The traditional debate has been whether the Return of Christ comes before the Millennium (premillennial) or afterwards (postmillennial). The different views might also be classified by their timing of the binding of Satan. Augustine's view, and mine, is that Satan has been bound. Conceiving the Millennium to be an ideal state of affairs, the premillennialists have concluded that Satan *will be* bound, in all the powers which have become associated with him. In Victorian times, the postmillennial proposal was that Satan *"is being bound"* by the advance of the gospel, It seemed plausible, in that era, that mission work would spread the gospel all over the globe and create an approximation of an ideal world. It seems to me, though, that their approach was turning a blind eye to what Revelation says about tribulation and catastrophe.

In this labelling scheme, many people would call Augustine "amillennial" ("no Millennium"); a little unfairly, because he does believe in a Millennium (by a less idealistic definition), and places the Return of Christ at the end of it, making him a true postmillennial.

V4 "Then I saw thrones, and seated on them were those to whom judgement was committed. Also I saw the souls of those who had been beheaded for their testimony to Jesus… They came back to life and reigned with Christ a thousand years."

The martyrs are given special attention, but the word "also" suggests that they are a distinct group, or at least a sub-category of the larger group. "If we endure, we shall also reign with him" (2 Timothy ch2 v12), the criterion being faithfulness rather than martyrdom as such. Paul also speaks of the sitting in judgement; "Do you not know that the saints will judge the world?" (1 Corinthians ch6 v2).

Similar statements are found elsewhere in the New Testament about Christians in general. Ephesians tells us that we are already sitting "with [Christ] in the heavenly places" (Ephesians ch2 v6). Jesus says "He who hears my words, and believes him who sent me, has eternal life; he does not come into judgement, but has passed from death into life" (John ch5 v24). The implication is that after our earthly deaths we would simply continue sitting in the heavenly places, and "come back to life" looks like another way of saying the same thing.

Hence the ambiguity in 1Thessalonians about the return of those who have "died in Christ". Paul tells us, on the one hand, that they will be "raised first", and on the other hand that God will bring them "with" Jesus when he returns (1 Thessalonians ch4 vv14-16). I see no reason, then, to separate "the reign of the saints" from the *present* reign of Christ, though this reign has not yet been "revealed" to the world.

Vv5-6 "The rest of the dead did not come back to life until the thousand years were ended. This is the first resurrection. Blessed and holy is he who shares in the first resurrection. Over such the second death has no power"

The simplest way to reconcile these words with my understanding of the previous verse is on the premise that "the rest of the dead" are those who do not die "in the Lord". Then this blessing would be identical with the blessing already promised to those "who die in the Lord henceforth" (ch14 v13). "He who conquers" has already been told that he will not be hurt by the second death (ch2 v11), and the promise is clearly applicable to everyone whose names are written in the book of life (v15, and ch3 v5).

Vv7-8 "And when the thousand years are ended, Satan will be loosed form his prison… to deceive the nations which are at the four corners of the world, that is, Gog and Magog."

This is an echo of, and an interpretation of, the prophecy against "Gog of the land of Magog" (Ezekiel chs38&39). The mutation of "Gog from Magog" into "Gog and Magog" should make us cautious about holding on to literal details. The prophecy looks forward to a time when God's people have been living in peace and safety. Then Gog's malice will drive him (and God, for his own purposes, will lead him) into coming out and attacking them. The outcome will be his party's final defeat and God's final victory.

In my scheme of interpretation, the security of God's people in Ezekiel, and the Millennium in this chapter, represent the long interval since Constantine's time without a *general* persecution of the Christian community. Then this fresh attack by the peoples of the world indicates a renewal of the state of tribulation. In other words, I suggest, the events of the previous chapters would be repeated, perhaps beginning with the Four Horsemen, and culminating once more in God's triumphal act of salvation. This time round, the story would be completed by the final catastrophe of the Trumpets and Bowls, which had no place in the original tribulation. That is the proposition summed up in these verses by the image of the besieged camp and the fire from heaven.


V11 "Then I saw a great white throne and him who sat upon it; from his presence earth and sky fled away."

This is an echo of the judgement scene in Daniel ch7. 2 Peter has a more dramatic description of the "flight" of the world; "But the day of the Lord will come like a thief, and then the heavens will pass away with a loud noise, and the elements will be dissolved with fire, and the earth and the works that are upon it will be burned up" (2 Peter ch3 v10).

In the rest of the New Testament, the effects of the Return of Christ follow on immediately from the Return of Christ. Thus the dissolution of the present world in the last-mentioned verse. Thus the general judgement; "When the Son of man comes in his glory and all the angels with him, then he will sit on his glorious throne" (Matthew ch25 v31). Thus the gathering of God's people into the eternal presence of their God; "We shall be caught up… to meet the Lord in the air; and so we shall be always with the Lord" (1 Thessalonians ch4 v17). Only in Revelation is there an apparent interval between the Return of Christ and its consequences. So anyone who insists on a literal interval is defying the authority of the rest of the New Testament.

This difficulty, too, is overcome by the distinction between the John's message to his own time and his message for the future church.. Yes, the Millennium follows on from God's triumph in ch19, but it follows on from the "first message" version of that triumph. That is, it follows the victories of Constantine and indicates the existence of a gap between the two sets of tribulation. The "second message" version of that event would be the Return of Christ, and then there would be no second interval before this time of judgement.

V12 "Books were opened. Also another book was opened, which is the book of life. And the dead were judged by what was written in the books, by what they had done."

This looks like a two-stage process, using two sets of records. The books first mentioned, the multiple books, were opened in Daniel's judgement scene (Daniel ch7 v10) These provide the judgement by deeds, under which, presumably, everyone stands condemned in the eyes of God; "There is none righteous, no not one" (Romans ch3 v10). Then the single book is opened, the Lamb's book of life; "At that time your people shall be delivered, every one whose name shall be found written in the book" (Daniel ch12 v1) In this chapter, those whose names are in the book are exempt from the condemnation and escape the lake of fire. So this imagery is expressing Paul's teaching that we are saved "in Christ" from the wrath of God, and not by our own works.

Anyone whose name is not written in the book of life will suffer "the second death", being thrown into the lake of fire along with Death and Hades. Now Death and Hades are abstractions. This means that the lake of fire cannot be understood as "eternal torment", despite the statement of v10, because abstractions cannot be tormented. The real significance of the image must be that we cease to be acquainted with Death and Hades, and perhaps we should understand the fate of the persecutors and "those not written in the book of life" in the same way.

We may compare Paul's teaching about the effects of Christ's Return. He says that those who do not know God "shall suffer the punishment of eternal destruction (OLETHRON) and exclusion from the presence of the Lord" (2 Thessalonians ch1 v9). The image found in the teaching of Jesus is the "outer darkness", where "men shall weep and gnash their teeth" (Matthew ch25 v30). We know, then, that their fate is less preferable than being in the presence of God, but we hardly know more than that. The message for this chapter is that all these things cease to have a presence in God's world, and therefore cease to be part of the experience of God's people. That is the main sense in which they are "destroyed".

# 19

# THE NEW JERUSALEM

## (Revelation Chapters 21&22)

Paul says "So we shall be always with the Lord" (2 Thessalonians ch4 v17). These last two chapters will be offering a series of metaphors to express that fundamental teaching.

V1 "Then I saw a new heaven and a new earth; for the first heaven and the first earth had passed away, and the sea was no more."

The new heavens and the new earth were promised in Isaiah ch66 v22. The God of Revelation is the Creator God, and the climax of his work is a renovation of the created world which amounts to a new creation, To be exact, as he confirms in v5, two of the three regions of the created world have been renewed. Their old versions have simply "passed away" [APELTHON]. But the sea "is not, any longer" [OUK ESTIN ETI], an expression which links it verbally with the Beast from the sea, who "is not" (ch17 v8). The sea must go, symbolically, because it represents what lies outside God's will. There will be no "reservoir" to supply fresh evils to the world.

V2 "And I saw the holy city, new Jerusalem... prepared as a bride adorned for her husband."

We find in Galatians a contrast between the "present" or literal Jerusalem, and "the Jerusalem above" who is "our mother". Her status as a bride fulfils the promise made by the Lord about the time when his people have been reconciled; "I will betroth you to me for ever; I will betroth you to me in righteousness and in justice, in steadfast love and in mercy" (Hosea ch2 v19).

It also matches the position of the Church; For Christ loved the church, and sanctified it, "that he might present the church to himself in splendour...that she might be holy and without blemish." (Ephesians ch5 vv25-27). Evidently "Jerusalem" represents the coming together of God's people, a community last seen as "the woman in heaven" in ch12.

The next part of the teaching is about God's presence with his people, and what this means for them.

V3 "Behold, the dwelling of God is with men. He will dwell with them and they shall be his people."

This echoes almost exactly the promise in Ezekiel; "My dwelling-place shall be with them, and I will be their God, and they shall be my people" (Ezekiel ch37 v37).

V4 "He will wipe away every tear from their eyes, and death shall be no more, neither shall there be mourning nor crying nor pain any more".

The effect of God's presence is the absence of evil things. This may be compared with the promises in Isaiah; "He shall swallow up death for ever, and the Lord God shall wipe away tears from all eyes" (Isaiah ch25 v8), and again; "They shall obtain joy and gladness, and sorrow and mourning shall flee away" (Isaiah ch38 v14).

The throne in these chapters is called "the throne of God and of the Lamb" (ch22 v1) It's almost impossible to separate them, especially in the following verses, because they seem to be speaking with the same voice.

V5 "Behold, I make all things new."

This declaration can only belong to the God who made the world in the first place.

"For these words [LOGOI] are trustworthy and true."

But this expression [PISTOS KAI ALETHINOS] has been used already as one of the title of Christ, and is combined with LOGOS in his descent from heaven (ch19 vv11-13).

V6 "It is done!"

There's a resemblance in thought between this exclamation and "It is finished!", the last word Jesus spoke on the Cross. Very appropriately, for we learned in ch5 how the Cross was the key event which made all these things possible.

*"I am the Alpha and the Omega, the beginning and the end"*

The same claim will be repeated by that Jesus who is "coming soon" (ch22 v12), but these titles were first applied to the Lord God Almighty (ch1 v8).

*"To the thirsty I will give from the fountain of the water of life without payment."*

This promise is based partly on the Lord's "without price" offer to everyone who thirsts (Isaiah ch55 v1), and partly on the gospel offer of "a spring of water welling up to eternal life" (John ch4 v14).

V7 "He who conquers shall have this heritage, and I will be his God, and he will be my son."

The first half of that promise echoes the refrain of Jesus in the letters to the churches, but the second half shows that the offer comes ultimately from the Father. Our heritage is that we are adopted sons, and daughters, because we belong to the Son (Galatians ch4 vv4-5). Thus we find ourselves included in the "You are my son" promise of Psalm 2 v7.

There is a list of natures excluded from this heritage. At the top of the list, perhaps because they failed to resist the Beast, are the cowardly and the faithless [APISTOI]. These are the exact opposite of the qualities "faithful and true", which belong to God and his Christ. The rest of the list partly resembles Paul's list of those who will not "inherit the kingdom of God" (1 Corinthians ch6 v9). These are all different ways of failing to "conquer".

The next stage in the vision echoes the great "temple" vision at the end of Ezekiel, from ch40. Both visions are about the renewed presence of God with his people. Once again, there are differences in detail which should caution us against taking either set of details as a literal picture.

This vision, like the vision of the Harlot in ch17, is introduced by one of the seven angels who carried the bowls of the final plague. This underlines the point that the new Jerusalem and the Harlot are polar opposites, the faithful and the unfaithful versions of God's people. As in Ezekiel, John is taken up a high mountain and sees a structure like a city. He then watches while the structure is measured (we had one version of this at the beginning of ch11).

In this case, the measurements are based on the same symbolic numbers that were used in the sealing of the servants of God (ch7). The number 12 is dominant, the number of God's people. There are 12 gates, labelled with the names of the twelve tribes, and 12 foundations, labelled with the names of the twelve apostles. The measurement of the protective wall around the city is 144 cubits, the square of 12. The equivalent measure in Ezekiel applies both to the height and to the thickness of the wall. The other significant number is 1000, which I understand as God's version of 10- not just the full extent of the world, but the full extent of God's world. Thus the measurement of the city itself is 12,000 stadia- that is, 12 multiplied by 1000.. That number is then cubed again, because it applies to the length and to the breadth and to the height of the city.

My interpretation of these measurements is "God's people, in perfection, occupying the absolute fullness of God's world."

The construction of the city is very ornate, with streets of gold, gates of pearl, and precious stones of every kind in the foundations. I can leave it to other people to find symbolism in the individual stones.

The point is that the appearance of the city is overwhelmingly glorious, helping to fulfil the prophetic assurance (see below) that the old glories of Jerusalem would be restored.

V22 "And I saw no temple in the city, for its temple is the Lord God Almighty and the Lamb."

Correcting the vision of Ezekiel. The direct presence of God does not need an intervening temple, even in a symbolic description.

V23 "And the city has no need of sun or moon to shine upon it, for the glory of God is its light, and its lamp is the Lamb."

This rewords the promise of Isaiah; "The sun shall be no more your light by day, nor for brightness shall the moon be your light by night; but the Lord shall be your everlasting light and your God shall be your glory" (Isaiah ch60 vv19-20).

Vv24-26 "The kings of the earth shall bring their glory into it, and its gates will never be shut by day- and there shall be no night there; they shall bring into it the glory and the honour of the nations."

The historical experience of Jerusalem was that nations and their kings had been taking wealth away from Jerusalem. These verses are a rewording of Isaiah's promise that the process would be reversed; "Your gates shall be open continually, day and night they shall not be shut; that men may bring to you the wealth of the nations with their kings led in procession" (Isaiah ch60 v11). The vision of this chapter represents the fulfilment, though in symbolic ways, of everything that God has ever promised to his people.

V27 "But nothing unclean shall enter it, nor anyone who practices abomination or falsehood."

These three exclusions are essentially about the worship of other gods. This is a place which acknowledges the Creator God alone. However, these verses are not really telling us that there is an "outside" where the unclean are still dwelling. The new Jerusalem is the world, and in that world nothing unclean will exist.

Finally (as we move into the last chapter), the centre of the city is occupied by an image, or a combination of images, relating to Life.

Ch22 v1 "Then he showed me the river of the water of life… lowing from the throne of God and of the Lamb."

This image is based mainly on the stream that flows in Ezekiel ch47, flowing from the threshold of the temple. In the prophet's vision, it becomes a great river, giving life everywhere it goes, with trees growing on either side.

V2 "Also, on either side of the river, the tree of life."

The natural reading, at first glance, is that the river must flow through a natural arch in the middle of the tree. This bizarre picture (I've seen the illustrations) disappears if we take our cue from Ezekiel and suppose that the *species* "tree of Life" grows on both banks.

In order to understand this tree of Life, we must first understand the original tree of Life. This tree was planted "in the midst of the garden" for the benefit of Adam and Eve (Genesis ch2 v9) because it was absolutely central to their existence in the garden. The whole point and purpose of the garden was that they should be eating from the tree, and they would have been eating regularly until they were expelled. The modern perception that the tree is a puzzle and something of an anomaly springs out of the false analogy with the *single* eating from the tree of knowledge. As metaphors, the garden is about direct contact with God, and this tree is about drawing Life direct from God. They go together, necessarily.

The crisis in the garden, when men chose to follow their own will instead of God's will, brought down a barrier between God and man. The Atonement, when the Son followed his Father's will, broke through that barrier and brought us back into the presence of God. That is the meaning of these final chapters. In effect, the new Jerusalem is a restoration of the garden, and brings with it a restoration of the tree of Life.

The tree is yielding fruit all through the twelve months of the year. That is, for the benefit of God's people, and also continuously. The true Life from God will never be inaccessible again. Which shows, incidentally, that John's understanding of the tree is the same as mine- a single eating of the fruit is not enough.

Now that the Bible has come round full circle in this way, the message of Revelation is complete. The remainder of the final chapter is almost redundant, and may be surveyed more rapidly.

V3 "There shall no more be anything accursed."

This fulfils the prophetic promise; "And it shall be inhabited, there shall be no more curse; Jerusalem shall dwell in security" (Zechariah ch14 v11).

At the same time, it revokes the curse imposed after the events in Eden (Genesis ch3).

V4 "They shall see his face".

Another aspect of cancelling the curse of Genesis. This is the face from which Adam hid in the garden.


V5 "They shall reign for ever and ever."

We may compare "The saints of the Most High shall receive the kingdom, and possess the kingdom for ever, for ever and ever" (Daniel ch7 v18).

We are brought back to Jesus, in vv6-7, with echoes of the first three verses of the book.. I've already remarked on the statement "These words are trustworthy and true". In the opening verse of Revelation, Jesus declared that he was sending his angel to show his servants what must soon take place. The declaration is repeated here, with a significant change; the word "I" is replaced by "The Lord, the God of the spirits of the prophets". Nevertheless, the following "Behold I am coming soon" must be a promise from Jesus himself (compare ch1 v7 and ch16 v15).

Since the words of prophecy have now been read, the blessing is offered to those who keep them (omitting the anticipatory blessings on those who read and hear). Finally, as in the opening chapter, John identifies himself as the first recipient of the message.

There follows, in vv8-9, a repetition of the "misdirected worship" incident of ch19. The phrase "who hold the testimony of Jesus" is replaced by "who keep the words of this book", In other words, the Christian gospel is at the heart of the book of Revelation and inseparable from it.


Vv10-11 "And he said to me; Do not seal up the words of the prophecy of this book, for the time is near. Let the evildoer still do evil, and the filthy still be filthy, and the righteous still do right, and the holy still be holy."

This needs to be recognised as the "updating" of similar passages in Daniel; "But you, Daniel, shut up the words and seal the book, until the time of the end. Many shall run to and fro and knowledge shall increase" (Daniel ch12 v4). And again; "The words are shut up and sealed until the time of the end. Many shall purify themselves and make themselves white and be refined; but the wicked shall do wickedly" (Daniel ch12 vv9-10).

Here Daniel and Revelation help to explain each other. It is easy enough to see that the order to "seal" has now been reversed. Taken in isolation, the latter part of the first Daniel passage is more obscure. What kind of knowledge? Does "run to and fro" refer to the modern railway system, as proposed by one of Tolstoy's characters? But a comparison with Revelation brings out the contrast between "settled" and "unsettled". Daniel sees people continuing to waver between righteousness and unrighteousness, though the trend is towards an increasing knowledge of God. When we reach "the time of the end", there is no more indecision. They have made their choice, one way or the other, between what is holy and what is not holy.

V12 "Behold I am coming soon, bringing my recompense."
"Behold, the Lord God comes with might, and his arm rules for him; behold, his reward is with him, and his recompense before him" (Isaiah ch40 v10).

V13 "I am the Alpha and the Omega, the beginning and the end, the first and the last."
The angel of Jesus is still speaking. As these three statements are brought together, it's worth remembering where they've been used before. The first was applied to the Lord God Almighty (ch1 v8).The second was the self-description of Jesus (ch1 v17, ch2 v8), while the other two are combined for the ambiguous figure "who sat upon the throne" (ch21 v6). There is no clear boundary between God and the Lamb, and that is how, in symbolism, Revelation presents the New Testament doctrine of the Incarnation.

V14 "Blessed are those who wash their robes."
That is, their sins have been forgiven. This verse ties up a loose end, confirming that the great heavenly crowd seen previously have become the community of the new Jerusalem.

V16 "I am the root and offspring of David, the bright morning star."

The first clause is an echo of Isaiah; "There shall come forth a shoot from the root of Jesse, and a branch shall grow out of his roots" (Isaiah ch11 v1). He's already promised to give "the morning star" to those who conquer (ch2 v28), and there may be an allusion to "A star shall come out of Jacob and a sceptre shall arise out of Israel" (Numbers ch24 v17). I like the idea that he is the root of David for the Old Testament, the offspring of David for the New Testament, and the morning star for the age to come.

Foolishly ingenious people have claimed that "Jesus claims identity with Lucifer", referring to Isaiah ch14 v12. I'll just make a couple of observations on that point. One is that the "Lucifer" reading of the Isaiah verse is very dubious, since the chapter as a whole is clearly addressed to the king of Babylon. The other is that "morning star" is a title of honour, not a name. Titles of honour can be shared by more than one person, just as Jesus already shares the title of "king" with Nebuchadnezzar.

V17, v20 "The Spirit and the Bride say 'Come'. And let him who hears say 'Come'. And let him who is thirsty come..."

*"He who testifies to these things says 'Surely I am coming soon' Amen, come Lord Jesus."*

The first invitation is addressed to Jesus, urging him to return. The Bride is the church, of course. The Spirit and the Bride must speak together, because the Spirit addresses the world through the church and the church addresses God through the Spirit. They have one voice. Then those who hear or read these visions are invited to join in the call to Christ. The third invitation picks up the word " come", addressing it in the reverse direction. If we want God to come to us, we must be willing to come to God. Finally, Jesus responds to the original invitation by confirming his promise. Jesus has already identified himself as "the Amen, the faithful and true witness" (ch3 v14).

The warnings of vv18-19 about changing the wording of this vision are not just addressed to errant copyists. "You shall not add to the word which I command you, nor take from it" (Deuteronomy ch4 v2). Moses was establishing a covenant, and I've already suggested that the angel of ch10 was announcing the arrival of a new covenant.

The end of Revelation is the final consummation of the work that was achieved on the Cross. God and mankind are at peace. If there is peace between earth and heaven, then God's wrath has been removed from the world. If God's wrath has been removed from the world, then that is what is meant by "Silence in heaven".

# 20

# DANIEL'S WEEK
# AND
# REVELATION'S HOUR

Someone told me, when I was at school, that the first sign of madness was having hair on the palm of the hand. And the second sign was looking for it. "Believing that you understand the book of Revelation" would also come high on the list, in popular opinion.

My claim to be offering a saner approach to this book is based partly on the fact that my futurist interpretations are genuinely futurist. That is, I'm not obsessed with finding detailed fulfilment of Revelation in current events, in order to be at the centre of the experience. In these final pages, I allow myself some cautious speculation around the text of Revelation, to the extent that it seems reasonable.

My first step is to look for correlations between the apparent timeline of this Revelation crisis and the similar crisis described in the last chapters of Daniel. Revelation's picture of the future is painted with a broad brush, but it can't be called a "timeless" allegory. There is a narrative sequence with a clear storyline, which can be discovered once we get past the obscure descriptions and the disjointed chronology. Then it can be matched against the sketchy storyline found in Daniel.

We can begin with the "seventy weeks of years" of Daniel ch9, culminating in "the prince who is to come". Daniel says that the prince will be dominant for "one week", or seven years. There is a great change in the middle of the this period, because he "shall cause offering and sacrifice to cease" (preventing the worship of God) The event is echoed in Daniel ch11 v31, where a king's forces ""take away the continual burnt offering" and also "set up the abomination that makes desolate". All this brings trouble in the second half of the week, and the implication is that the first half-week is untroubled.

Then in Daniel ch12 an angel announces that "the end of these wonders" will come after the passage of "a time, two times, and half a time". This adds up to "three and a half times" and can be equated with "half a week". At the end of this period the "shattering of the power of the holy people" will come to an end, so it obviously relates to the second half-week, when they're under the prince's power.

When we come to Revelation, we find that most of the time-periods mentioned are different versions of that same "half-week". Thus the Beast is "allowed to exercise authority" for a period of forty-two months, or three and a half years (ch13 v5). The nations are " trampling over the holy city" for the same period (ch11 v2). The two witnesses in the next verse are giving their testimony for a period of one thousand, two hundred and sixty days- which is forty-two months, taken at thirty days per month. Their dead bodies are left in the open for three and a half days. I make that half a week. Finally, the "woman" who represents God's people will be "nourished in the wilderness" for a period which is described both as "one thousand, two hundred and sixty days" (ch12 v6) and also as "a time, two times, and half a time" (ch12 v14).

The natural assumption is that these are all different ways of describing the same period, which means that all these events can be correlated. This period when the Beast "makes war on the saints" is the Revelation equivalent of that period when Daniel's prince stops the worship of God.

There's another set of time-references which needs to be brought into the picture. There is the "one hour" during which the Beast and the ten kings are ruling (ch17 v12) and the "half an hour" of the silence in heaven (ch8 v1). I've already argued that the silence is the "peaceful" first half of the full hour, leaving the second half to be occupied by the "war on the saints".

I've shown that Daniel's prince rules for "one week", divided into a peaceful first half and a war-troubled second half. The Beast rules for "one hour", divided into a peaceful first half and a war-troubled second half. Thus we can take the week and the hour as alternative labels for the same time-span, and the timeline of Revelation begins to fall into place.

*The prelude*

The first six chapters of Revelation cover the period immediately *before* the "hour" starts. The first event in this period of history is a persecution of God's people. It's part of the background of ch1 ("who share with you in Jesus the tribulation and the kingdom and the patient endurance"). The martyred victims of this persecution are the souls who are seen "under the altar" when the fifth seal is opened. I interpreted the events of ch6 as God's response to this persecution. Then, at the beginning of ch7, God restrains his agents of judgement, "the four winds of the earth". In other words, God calls a truce. The martyrs of the first persecution must be joined (as they've already been told) by the martyrs of a further persecution, and preparations must be made on both sides.

*First half-week- "The truce"*

What the Beast does during the truce

This will be the time when the Beast is establishing its power. The Four Horsemen episode has just come to an end. I've proposed that episode as the "mortal wound" from which the Beast from the sea (the political state) makes a dramatic recovery, thus providing leadership to the world as the rest of the world recovers.

We're told in Daniel that the prince "shall make a strong covenant with many" for the whole period of one week. We're told here, in ch17, that the ten kings "give over their power and authority to the Beast", so that they rule together for the one hour. Once again, bringing the two statements together makes them evident as two different ways of describing the same thing. The Beast is able to dominate the world, directly or indirectly, through its arrangements with lesser powers. "And authority was given it over every tribe and people and tongue and nation".

*What God does during the truce*

God's purpose in calling the truce (as announced in ch7) is to make time for the "sealing" of his servants. The whole of the period is available for this operation. Apart from that, it is the period of the "silence in heaven", as already mentioned, the period when God is *not* expressing his full wrath upon the earth.

*Half-way point- "The transition"*
*What the Beast does at the transition*

In Daniel, the beginning of the prince's "war with God" is clearly marked. "They shall set up the abomination which makes desolate", and the second half-week is the period when "he shall cause sacrifice and offering to cease". In Revelation, the Beast's war on God and the saints follows the time of truce, but no event is named as the starting-point. I'll be coming back to that question.

*What God does at the transition*

But the reaction from the other side is very clearly marked, in the first few verses of ch8.An angel comes forward with incense which represents the renewed "prayers of the saints", which are presumably an appeal against what the Beast is now doing. God's response to these prayers is the very noisy demonstration of wrath showing his determination to deal with the Beast. So that is the end of the silence.

*Second half-week- "The war"*
*What the Beast does during the war*

This period is defined by the Beast's active hostility towards God and his people. The Beast is dominating the world, and "trampling over the holy city". God's people are reduced to a kind of underground existence, "nourished in the wilderness", while the "two witnesses", another aspect of God's people, will be giving their testimony and getting themselves killed.

*What God does during the war*

This is the period of the "seven trumpets" and "seven vials", which culminate in the final destruction of the Beast and the Return of Christ.

Now what about the act that breaks the truce? What kind of event could be an "abomination of desolation" (which is also predicted in Matthew ch24)? To understand that phrase correctly, we need to focus on the true meaning of those two words.

*What is meant by "abomination"?*

The Hebrew version of this word is found many times in the Old Testament. I think the real heart of the concept can be found in the thought expressed in Deuteronomy ch13 vv13-14, where the name
is applied to the proposal "let us go and serve other gods". God's first and primary directive to his people was "You shall have no other gods but me". Anything that breaks that command is offensive to God, and so might be called an "abomination".

The term is used for the gods of other nations- "Milcom, the abomination of the Ammonites" (1 Kings ch11 v5). It includes the idols associated with their worship- "Cursed be the man who makes a graven or a molten image, an abomination to the Lord" (Deuteronomy ch27 v15). For that matter, it includes anything else that has been associated with the worship of other gods- gold or silver stripped from their statues, or money brought in from sacred prostitution (Deuteronomy ch23 v18).

The meaning of the English word is that something is detestable or loathsome. In modern translations, we may find the phrase "disgusting thing", which expresses a similar meaning more clumsily, and slightly weakens it. Anyway, the word is expressing God's forceful rejection of idolatry and idolatrous behaviour, a reaction which he wants his people to share.

*What is meant by "desolation"?*

The Hebrew version of this word goes back to a verb which means "to be desolate, laid waste". In some cases, like Ezra ch9 v3, translated as "astonished"- perhaps because the person's ability to think has been "laid waste".

The English word "desolation" comes ultimately from the Latin SOLUS- "alone". It describes loneliness or bereavement or a sense of having been abandoned. The derivation of the English word doesn't tell us anything directly about the meaning of the Hebrew, but in this case we've also got a Greek translation.

The Greek version of the phrase "abomination of desolation" is found in 1 Maccabees, in the Septuagint translation of Daniel, and in the gospel accounts. The basic meaning of the word used to translate the second part of the phrase is "made uninhabited", and it comes ultimately from EREMOS- which, again, means "alone". This is important, because these passages were written by Jews, who obviously accepted that word as the best rendering of their understanding of the Hebrew. This gives us good reason to understand "loneliness" as the real heart of the concept.

## *How does the Abomination bring desolation?*

When Antiochus Epiphanes set up an image of Jupiter in the Temple at Jerusalem, this was described in Maccabees as "an abomination of desolation". It's been suggested that this phrase is a deliberate distortion of the title ("Baal of heaven") which he would have given to the image. Even if this is true, the words which were chosen for the distortion still have a meaning, and it's still worth considering why they seemed appropriate.

Obviously the image was an "abomination" because it offered an alternative object of worship, but in what sense did it bring "desolation"? One common understanding links "desolation" to the wars that follow the event in the Maccabean histories, and the equivalent troubles described in Daniel and in Matthew ch24. This view is encouraged by Daniel ch9 v26, which associates "desolations" (in the plural) with war. But it seems to me, examining the passages closely, that when the abomination "makes desolate," in Daniel ch9 v27 and ch11 v31, this is an immediate effect, and something distinct from the wars described in the surrounding verses.

It's possible to find a much more direct connection between "abomination" and "desolation" if we focus on the idea that "desolation" is about loneliness and loss of contact. To the Jewish people of the time, the Temple in Jerusalem was the primary contact point between the nation and their God, and the continual sacrifice was the primary means of contact. But the king had "stopped the sacrifices" (or diverted them towards his own image, which comes to the same thing). This had the appearance of breaking the contact between the Jewish nation and their God, leaving them bereft and isolated. And *that*, I suggest, is what is meant by "making desolate". Not a delayed effect, but the immediate consequence of setting up the image.

In that case, we can take the view that" abomination" and "desolation" are two different aspects of one and the same event. The great sacrilege becomes an "abomination" by presenting an alternative object of worship. At the same time, it makes a "desolation" by displacing the customary and legitimate worship, on which the people have been depending. To put it another way, "abomination" describes God's own judgement on the sacrilege, and "desolation" describes how the same sacrilege is experienced by God's people.

*How might the Beast establish an abomination that brings desolation?*
Let us suppose that the Beast is claiming, as many people expect him to claim, to be in some sense the returned Christ. This would be the individual Beast, of course, the one "from the land". If he held enough power in the world, he would be in a position to insist on getting that claim acknowledged by the publicly organised churches. He would want them to incorporate it into their doctrinal statements, their public worship, their teaching, and their public life in general. There would be no need for a statue or any other image (though he might find some symbol to replace the cross). That would be enough to constitute an "abomination".

And there is also a regular activity which he could "cause to cease". The Lord's Supper is not a sacrifice, of course, in Paul's teaching, but it is a contact-point with God. It is a fellowship meal, at which Christ is present in some way which need not be defined.

Paul tells us that eating the Lord's Supper is a way of proclaiming his death "until he comes" (1 Corinthians ch11 v26). Anyone claiming to be the returned Christ should be expected (it would be a logical obligation) to take exception to that premise; "I'm here now, we don't need that any more". The celebration of the Supper in those terms would have to come to an end. It would only be permitted, if at all, in a remodelled version which acknowledged his claim. If such a change were forced upon churches, as public bodies, then the true point of contact would be lost, and that would be enough to constitute a "desolation".

No doubt the genuine tradition of the Lord's Supper would be preserved, but it would be preserved under conditions of danger and secrecy. The celebrants would be at odds with the political authorities.

Their neighbours would call the police complaining that the party next door was too quiet; "They say it's an orgy, but we think it might be a surreptitious prayer meeting." They would also be at odds with their own church authorities, which could only exist by permission of the state.

The result would be chaos and confusion in the churches. The boundary-line between "faithful" and "unfaithful" would run between individuals, not between denominations. Which of your Christian brethren could you invite to a secret meeting without fearing that they would give you away? It would be a crisis calling for the patience and endurance of the saints.

# 21

# BLIND ALLEYS

Ever since Martin Luther's time, it has been traditional to identify the Papacy with the Beast. Unfortunately it has also been traditional to identify the Papacy with the Harlot of Babylon. Careful reading of ch17 shows that the Beast and the Harlot are distinct entities, sometimes in alliance and sometimes in conflict, so that the same institution cannot represent both of them. I would have thought, myself, that the Harlot, as a religious establishment resting on the general support of the political establishment, would make a better match.

At least there was a logic in Luther's theory at the time, because a persecution of Christians was taking place. Revelation is a book about the impact of persecution, and the hostile figures in the book represent the persecutors. The bane of modern popular interpretation of Revelation is the earnest desire to see Revelation fulfilled in the reader's own generation, which entails ignoring those basic truths. The result is a fervent speculation which revolves around other ways of fixing their identities.

Of course the number of the Beast is thought to be an important sign. The invitation to calculate the number is rightly understood as a reference to the use of gematria, but we must distinguish between John's two messages. The God of the Bible is a communicating God, who wants himself to be understood. He does not speak through secret codes, leaving his meaning to be uncovered by code-breakers. He could reasonably expect the church of John's time to find Nero's name in that way, because there were so few imperial names to choose from. They used letters to represent numbers as a matter of course, and a code based on that habit would not be obscure to them. No more so than a code based on acronyms would be obscure to us ("… and there was a great king in the west whose name was UKUSANATO").

But why would he use that method to speak to people in the modern world, where we have lost the ability to make sense of it? This is not a language understood by the people at large. Enthusiasts have been obliged to invent their own versions of gematria to make it work at all. Even so, the system cannot give us a clear message. It cannot point us towards any unique name. Lord Macaulay met in India a man who found the number of the Beast in the name of Napoleon Bonaparte (spelling it in Arabic, and omitting two of the letters). That is the general practice in the examples that I've seen, viz. working backwards from the desired conclusion and "fudging" the calculation until it comes out right. Macaulay responded at the time by claiming to find the same number in the membership of the House of Commons.

So I'm convinced that the method can be used safely only in the way that I've already proposed; the calculation points towards "Nero" for the church of John's time, and towards "someone like Nero" for the rest of us.

The other sign that tempts the imagination is "the Mark of the Beast". There are certain clues in the text which ought to be controlling the search.

First, there is the timing of the Mark, which is very clear and very important. It *follows*, necessarily, the emergence of the Beast itself. When the second Beast is compelling the world to accept his authority and to worship the first Beast, that is when he requires the Mark as a deliberate sign of loyalty. It serves as a tool in the general persecution.

The location of the mark is another clue, but we need not be bound by the literal meaning of "right hand or forehead". I've already suggested a symbolic interpretation, that the "law" provided by the Beast is taking the place of God's law.

The form of the Mark is supposed to be the name of the Beast or the number of his name, but this may be telling us only that the wearers are linked in some way to the identity of the Beast. The link would have to be manifest, because the presence or absence of the Mark has a social consequence.

Of course there's also a spiritual consequence, in that God's wrath awaits those who prefer to give their loyalty to the Beast. This indicates a voluntary choice of some kind, a decision against God, which means that taking the Mark is not something which happens accidentally. We cannot be "tricked" into it, because that would not be a genuine test of loyalty.

The key point is that the Beast knows his followers, and they know themselves, by use of the Mark. In letting go of that guide-rope, a lot of popular speculation about the nature of the Mark is led astray by false reasoning. For example, the ultra-literal may get absurdly anxious about the accidental appearance of a literal 666.

Another line of thought is based on "the Beast gives everyone a number". This leads to the observation that numbers have been given to most of us in the modern world, as a way to identify us and distinguish between us. But the analogy is inaccurate; everyone in the text gets the *same* number, because the Mark is there to present the name of the Beast, not the names of the people wearing it.

Another is founded on the warning that "no one can buy or sell unless he has the mark". For me, as I've said, the connection is indirect; anyone who defies the Beast is penalised by restrictions and boycotts. But ingenious minds have discovered a more direct connection; the Mark is to be found in some form of money, without which one cannot "buy or sell". Of course this also brings in "receiving a number". The basic flaw in the theory is that there is no connection at all between the use of money and the choice between God and the Beast.

The same objection applies to the reasoning "The Mark is imposed upon us, so this thing which might be imposed (perhaps a microchip or a vaccine) must be the Mark". But again, this would not involve a conscious choice between God and the Beast. It could not be a genuine test of loyalty.

The truth is that we turn the Beast and his Mark into a mystery by looking for them at the wrong time. We know now that allegiance to Adolf Hitler was expressed by the use of the swastika and by the Nazi salute; "Anyone not wishing to come under suspicion of behaving in a consciously negative manner will therefore render the 'Hitler-greeting'" (German decree, 1933). But would anyone have guessed this in advance of his birth? When there is a great persecution of the church, the identity of the great persecutor, and the nature of the signs that identify his followers, will surely be obvious enough. Before then, we cannot know, and we don't need to know.

Popular speculation really began with attempts to fix a near-future date for the Return of Christ. More recently, for the Rapture. That was always a futile exercise, because there is no real reason to suppose that fixed dates with precise intervals were ever part of God's plan for these events. If he has not been poring over the timeline of history with a spiritual tape-measure and a year-planner, nothing is to be gained by attempting to second-guess his calculations. God tells us in Revelation that he will respond to the tribulation of the church, but he does not tell us when the tribulation will start.

I always feel that attempts to fix a date for the Return of Christ are a symptom of declining faith. Real faith would be content to wait patiently for these things to happen in their own good time and God's. They certainly serve as faith-killing exercises, because they constantly raise expectations which are constantly disappointed.

In 1975, the Jehovah's Witnesses were still talking about "within a generation of 1914", but I suspect they may have allowed themselves to forget that slogan. The duplicated leaflets of the prophet "Individualist", who intercepted me outside the college gate, claimed that the world crisis would come when the grand Russian army invaded Israel in 1973. But even they came with the added warning "Beware Jehovah's Witnesses-set you trap". All these calculations are a trap, because the Bible gives us no genuine information to support them.

Nor does the Bible support the modern expectation of a separate Rapture. The Rapture theory is based on a misunderstanding of Paul's promise that we shall be "caught up to meet the Lord in the air" (1 Thessalonians ch4 vv15-17) As frequently happens, the misunderstanding comes from taking statements in isolation and ignoring the context. In this case, the context is the final Return of Christ, which concludes the whole story known to us.

Jesus told his disciples, more than once, that they would face tribulation. Though he did promise that the days of tribulation would be cut short for the sake of the elect (Matthew ch24 v22), which in itself shows that the elect would still be there. The function of the book of Revelation is to promote and encourage their faithful endurance during the time of tribulation. If they were going to evade the tribulation instead, the book would not be necessary.

People ask me "Where do you see the church during the events described In Revelation?" The answer is that I see the church in ch7, getting sealed with the Holy Spirit and consequently joining Christ "in the heavenly places". I see the church in ch11, worshipping around the altar and witnessing for Christ. I see the church in ch13, coming under the persecution of the Beast. And I see the church enjoying the triumph of the Lamb in the final chapters, when he comes "to vindicate his people" (Luke ch18 v8).

So the "Rapture" teaching is unhelpful, because it distracts the church from settling down for the long haul of "patient endurance". If it's combined with the practice of date-calculation, and the event fails to take place on the expected date, then it also becomes a faith-killer. Its a teaching which offers the short-term excitement of anticipation, but the excitement comes at a cost.

We have a better chance of understanding the book of Revelation if we can overcome our impatience to see prophecy fulfilled.

*Stephen Disraeli*

# 22

# OUR MISTRESS GAIA

I see the Harlot of Babylon as a religious establishment, managing human-centred forms of religion, resting upon the support of a political establishment. A world-religion, or a world-alliance of religions, supplementing the "political religion" of the worship of the Beast. We may be able to guess what it would look like by projecting forward some of the current trends of modern culture.

There is the casual expectance of reincarnation ("I'll come back as…") which has become a feature of modern folk-religion. There is the fashionable understanding that "spirituality" means a focus on the *human* spirit and what the human spirit can achieve. The book "Jonathan Livingston Seagull", which expounds this philosophy, can be seen even on the bookshelves of thoughtless Christians. The fictional Jedi belief-system, which is developing into a half-serious cult, is one of the symptoms of a willingness to believe in the (human-centred) power of the dead.

Sun Myung Moon thought he had a recipe for uniting the traditional religions of the world under one leadership. "The Lord of the Second Advent, who comes as the central figure of Christianity, will also play the role of Buddha, whom Buddhists believe will come again, as well as the role of the "True man" whose appearance Confucianists anticipate, and "Chung Do Ryung' ("Herald of the Righteous Way") whom many Koreans expect to come. In addition, he will also play the role of the central figure whom all other religions await" (Sun Myung Moon, "Divine principle", ch5 section3- "Unification of Religions by Resurrection through Second Coming").

So the different religions would be united "at the top", in the same way that Queen Elizabeth unites the Commonwealth by having different roles in different countries. He also had a deceptively simple way to identify where this new Messiah would appear. That is, he was expected to come "from the East". Not from Japan, because of the Second World War. Not from China, because China is Communist. By the elimination of the other two candidates, that left Korea.

This recipe did not work in practice. He could entice individuals away from the main religious communities, but he could not entice the religious communities themselves. By definition, a figure acceptable to the Christians would not have been acceptable to the Jews and the Muslims, and so on. The different religions of the world could only be united under an "umbrella" without any previous, alienating, religious associations. What could play this role?

I suggest that we look to environmentalism. We may learn to call this "Climate Change". I've noticed that expression becoming the new, shortened label for what is, strictly speaking, the campaign *against* climate change, so that a young enthusiast may claim to "support Climate Change" without any sense of irony. Concern for the environment is becoming more prevalent in our culture. It is becoming a kind of "background" belief. Like most forms of political enthusiasm, it resembles religion in a growing intolerance towards opposition or non-participation. At the same time, scientific environmentalism offers no offence to traditional religions. That makes it a natural "umbrella" belief-system, capable of embracing religious communities in general.

But what happens when environmentalism ceases to be scientific? If there is any truth in the more pessimistic projections, the time will come when people begin to lose their trust in scientific solutions. In their despair, they are likely to turn to non-rational solutions. That could be when Climate Change develops into a more religious outlook. Belief in the power of nature would begin to approach the worship of the gods of nature, which was prevalent in the Roman world.

The concept of Gaia was put forward in our own time as a metaphor, a label to identify the completeness of this planet as an environment. But when a less rational generation was beginning to panic about the state of the world, we might expect to see a more conscious personification of Gaia, preparing the way for appeals to Gaia's power to help them survive

As a literal female figure, she would still be plausibly compatible with many of the religions of the world. In the Roman Catholic community, the company of different versions of Mary could be expanded, no doubt, by the addition of "Mary Gaia", with her own cult and local visions. The Beast from the land could be brought into the system by claiming to be the son of Gaia (and in that sense the returned Christ).

The trouble would come when the appeals for help were taking the form of religious practices, capable of being understood as involving the worship of Gaia. Faithful Christians, and probably others, would refuse to participate. Since the cult would be endorsed by the political establishment, they could, with some reason, identify any compulsory element as the Mark of the Beast. But their failure to participate would be intolerable to the world at large. If the disputed ceremonies were deemed necessary to ward off droughts, floods, volcanoes and earthquakes, anyone holding back and refusing to take part would be blamed for *causing* droughts, floods, volcanoes and earthquakes. The vengeance of the frightened world would be hysterical.

This would be a re-creation of the public hostility which the church experienced from the Roman Empire in Tertullian's time; "You insist on our being the causes of every public calamity or injury. If the Tiber has overflowed its banks, if the Nile has remained in its bed, if the sky has been still, or the earth has been in commotion, if death has made its devastations, or famine its afflictions, your cry immediately is; "This is the fault of the Christians!"... I suppose it is as despisers of your gods that we call down these strokes of theirs... You incur the chastisement of your gods because you are too slack in our extirpation" (Tertullian- "Ad Nationes", ch9). This was the popular motive for Christian persecution, just as the refusal to offer incense to the Emperor was the official reason. There was a flaw in the logic, as Tertullian pointed out; if the gods were angry with the Christians, why would they express that indirectly by punishing the rest of the world? But we must not expect rationalism in times of heightened emotion.

That is one possible explanation of the Harlot "drunk with the blood of the saints". Of course nobody should elevate these thoughts to the status of "prophecy". They are a forward projection from current events, and don't claim to be anything more.

The important point is that there will always be a challenge to God's authority. We do not need to know what form it will take. Our role is to be ready for it, in any form, through our commitment to "God and his Christ".

"Here is a call for the endurance and faith of the saints."

# BIBLE REFERENCE INDEX

This index lists the Biblical passages quoted or mentioned in the text, the second column indicating the chapters (of Revelation) in which I find reason to quote them.

*Deuteronomy*
Ch4 v2 Do not change the law   ch22
Ch6 v8 The mark of the Lord   ch7, ch13
Ch27 v15 Abominations   ch17

*Judges*
Ch2 vv11-14 The sins of Israel   ch6

*1 Kings*
Ch10 v9 Solomon-666   ch13
Ch11 v4 Solomon idolatry   ch13
Ch18 Calling down fire   ch13

*2 Kings*
Ch9 v22 Jezebel   ch2
Ch17 v7 The sins of Israel   ch6
Ch23 v29 Megiddo   ch16

*1 Chronicles*
Ch24 v4 Families of Levi   ch4

*Nehemiah*
Ch8 v12 Rejoicing in the law   ch11

*Job*
Ch2 v9 Curse God   ch16
Ch3 v8 Leviathan   ch12
Ch3 vv20-26 Wanting to die   ch9

*Psalms*
Ps 2 v2 Rage against the Lord   ch11
Ps 2v9 Rod of iron   ch2, ch12
Ps 8vv4-5 What is man?   ch4
Ps23 Shepherd   ch7
Ps 24v8 Lord of Hosts   ch19

*Jeremiah*

| | |
|---|---|
| Ch4 vv24-29 Earth quakes, men flee | ch6 |
| Ch4 v30 Harlot Jerusalem | ch17 |
| Ch4 v31 Jerusalem in travail | ch12 |
| Ch5 v14 My words a fire in your mouth | ch11 |
| Ch9 vv14-15 Wormwood | ch8 |
| Ch15 v2 Four fates | ch6, ch13 |
| Ch25 v10 Joys lost | ch18 |
| Ch25 v26 Cup of wrath | ch16 |
| Ch46 v8 Egypt sends a flood | ch12 |
| Ch49 v36 Four winds | ch4, ch6 |
| Ch50 v38 Babylon river dries up | ch16 |
| Ch51 v25 Babylon-burnt mountain | ch8 |
| Ch51 vv7-8 Babylon-cup of wrath | ch18 |
| Ch51 v9 Babylon's judgement reaches heaven | ch18 |
| Ch51 v45 Leave Babylon | ch18 |
| Ch51 v63 Dropping the stone | ch18 |

*Ezekiel*

| | |
|---|---|
| Ch1 Vision of God ch1, | ch4 |
| Ch3 Eating the scroll | ch10 |
| Ch5 vv16-17 Four fates | ch6 |
| Ch9 vv4-6 Marked for God | ch7 |
| Ch13 vv18-19 Trading in souls | ch18 |
| Ch14 v21 Four fates | ch6 |
| Ch16 Bride Israel | ch19 |
| Chs26&27 Tyre | ch18 |
| Ch37 v3 Thou knowest | ch7 |
| Ch37 v10 Rising to feet | ch11 |
| Ch37 v37 God dwells with his people | ch21 |
| Ch39 Gog of Magog | ch19, ch20 |
| Ch40 Measuring the Temple | ch11 |
| Ch43 The Lord returns to the Temple | ch11 ch21 |
| Ch47 The stream from the Temple | ch22 |

*Zechariah*

| | |
|---|---|
| Ch1 Four horses | ch6 |
| Ch3 Satan against Joshua | ch12 |
| Ch3 v9 White stone | ch2 |
| Ch4 v10 Seven eyes | ch1 |
| Ch4 v14 Olive trees | ch11 |
| Ch5 vv5-11 The woman of Wickedness | ch18 |
| Ch6 Four horses, four winds | ch6, ch7 |
| Ch12 v10 Mourning over the pierced one | ch1 |
| Ch14 v11 Dwell in security | ch22 |

*Malachi*

| | |
|---|---|
| Ch4v1 The day of burning | ch1 |

*New Testament*

*Matthew*

| | |
|---|---|
| Ch18 v6 Millstone | ch18 |
| Ch18 v10 Their angels are in Heaven | ch7 |
| Ch21 v5 Mounted on an ass | ch19 |
| Ch23v35 Guilt for bloodshed | ch18 |
| Ch24 vv23-26 False christs | ch12 |
| Ch24 v30 Christ comes in glory | ch19 |
| Ch24 v41 When the thief comes | ch16 |
| Ch25 v30 Outer darkness | ch20 |
| Ch25 v31 Son of man sits in judgement | ch20 |
| Ch26 26 v52 Will perish by the sword | ch15 |

*Mark*

| | |
|---|---|
| Ch3 v27 Strong man bound | ch20 |
| Ch4 v17 if anyone has an ear | ch13 |

*Luke*

Ch10 v18 Satan falling ch12

Ch14 v15 Blessed those who eat ch19

Ch21 v24 Jerusalem trodden by gentiles ch11

*John*

Ch1 v1 The Word ch19

Ch1 v29 Lamb takes away sin ch4, ch12

Ch4 v14 Spring of eternal life ch7, ch21

Ch5 v24 Believer has eternal Life ch20

Ch6 vv49-51 Living bread ch2

*Acts*

Ch17 v30 God calls world to repentance ch9

*Romans*

Ch5 vv1-2 Grace and peace ch1

Ch6 v10 None righteous ch20

Ch8 v1 No condemnation ch2

Ch13 v1 Rulers appointed by God ch13

*1 Corinthians*

Ch1 v8 The Day of our Lord Jesus Christ ch19

Ch2 v14 Not receiving from the Spirit ch14

Ch3 v5 Servant of God ch19

Ch3 v16 You are God's Temple ch11

Ch6 v2 We will judge the world ch20

Ch6 v9 Will not inherit the kingdom ch21

Ch 6 v12 Self-confidence ch2

Ch8 v1 Self-confidence ch2

Ch10 vv8-9,v20 Immorality ch2

Ch15 v22 In the twinkling of an eye ch19

*2 Corinthians*

Ch1 vv21-22 Sealed with the Spirit ch7

*Ephesians*

| | |
|---|---|
| Ch1 vv13-14 Sealed with the Spirit | ch7 |
| Ch2 v6 Sitting with Christ in Heaven | ch7, ch12, ch20 |
| Ch5 vv25-27 Bride of Christ | ch19, ch20 |

*Galatians*

| | |
|---|---|
| Ch3 v27 Clothed in Christ | ch16 |
| Ch4 vv4-5 Adopted son | ch2 |
| Ch4 vv25-26 Two Jerusalems | ch12 |

*1 Thessalonians*

| | |
|---|---|
| Ch1 v9 Eternal destruction | ch21 |
| Ch4 vv16-17 Rising to meet Christ | ch11, ch20 |
| Ch5 vv2-6 Like a thief | ch16 |

*2 Thessalonians*

| | |
|---|---|
| Ch1 v8 Jesus comes in judgement | ch19 |
| Ch2 v4 Man of sin | ch11 |
| Ch4 v13 Always with the Lord | ch21 |

*Philippians*

| | |
|---|---|
| Ch2 v10 Every knee shall bow | ch1 |

*2 Timothy*

| | |
|---|---|
| Ch2 v12 We shall reign | ch20 |

*Hebrews*

| | |
|---|---|
| Ch4 v10 Enter God's rest | ch14 |
| Ch4 v12 Word sharper than a sword | ch1 |

*1 Peter*

| | |
|---|---|
| Ch3 v10 Day of the Lord like a thief | ch16 |
| Ch3 v20 Eight in ark | ch17 |
| Ch5 v13 Those living in Babylon c | h14 |

\*\*\*\*\*\*\*\*\*\*\*\*\*\*\*\*\*\*\*\*\*\*\*\*\*\*\*\*\*\*\*\*\*\*\*\*\*\*\*\*\*\*\*\*\*\*\*\*\*\*\*\*\*\*\*\*

Stephen Diseaeli. is available for book interviews and personal appearances. For more information visit michaeledwinq.com

To purchase additional copies of this book, visit our bookstore website: www.advbookstore.com

Longwood, Florida, USA
"we bring dreams to life"™
www.advbookstore.com

*Stephen Disraeli*

Lightning Source UK Ltd.
Milton Keynes UK
UKHW020344260422
402021UK00005B/152